Contents

HODDER AND STOUGHTON

LONDON   SYDNEY   AUCKLAND   TORONTO

Acknowledgments

The author and publishers wish to thank the following for permission to reproduce copyright material: Martin Secker and Warburg Ltd for 'The eagle' from *The Poetical Works of Andrew Young* by Andrew Young; and Faber and Faber for 'The warm and the cold' from *Season Songs* by Ted Hughes and 'Death of a naturalist' and 'Personal helicon' from *Death of a Naturalist* by Seamus Heaney.

The author is grateful to all those many teachers who took part in the survey work so willingly, to their pupils who enjoyed the groupwork, and to those of my own students who helped—in particular Judith Gillett and Craig Robinson. Special thanks to Keith Postlethwaite and Nicholas Benton for their patient help with the computing and the final wordprocessing of the typescript.

This book is dedicated to Sue, Nicholas and Timothy.

British Library Cataloguing in Publication Data

Benton, Peter
  Pupil, teacher, poem.
  1. English literature—Study and teaching
  (Secondary)
  I. Title
  821'.007'12   PR33

  ISBN 0 340 38192 2

First published 1986

Copyright © 1986 P. Benton

Printed in Great Britain
for Hodder and Stoughton Educational
a division of Hodder and Stoughton Ltd, Mill Road
Dunton Green, Sevenoaks, Kent by

CHAPTER ONE

Problems of Rhetoric and Reality

Good poetry does undoubtedly tend to form the soul and character; it tends to beget a love of beauty and of truth in alliance together; it suggests, however indirectly, high and noble principles of action, it inspires the emotion so helpful in making principles operative. Hence its extreme importance to all of us; but in our elementary schools its importance seems to me at present quite extraordinary. (Matthew Arnold, *Report*, 1880)

I think it is not particularly important to read and discuss poetry in class with my pupils because poetry is a fairly abstruse art-form, and interest in and pursuit of poetry is a pretty rarefied activity . . . English teachers and *Guardian* readers in the main. — Lots of other activities I enjoy more and to which I personally attach more value. (English teacher, secondary school, 1982)

Over a quarter of a century ago, James Reeves in his book *Teaching Poetry*[1] expressed his unhappiness about the way in which the subject was generally approached in classrooms and sought, with characteristic enthusiasm, clarity and practical concern, to share his understanding of the value of reading and writing poetry in schools. A poet and teacher himself, Reeves was influenced by the insights of a succession of creative teachers and educationists: Lawrence, Herbert Read, Marian Richardson, and, perhaps most importantly at the time he was writing, Marjorie Hourd. His gentle fanaticism ('far from apologising for poetry, I am a fanatic for it') won, and continues to win, many converts. He was to become one of a number of powerful advocates of a movement which saw the reading and increasingly the writing of verse by children as being at the heart of their educational experience. His desire was to see 'children of twelve' writing 'not colourless, though perhaps grammatical, prose compositions . . . but rough, vigorous, lively, possibly ungrammatical and unrhythmical verse about — what? Anything and everything under the sun.'

Margaret Langdon's explanation of 'Intensive writing' in *Let The Children Write* (1961), Sybil Marshall's *An Experiment in Education* (1963), Alec Clegg's *The Excitement of Writing* (1964), several books by David

Holbrook ranging from *English for Maturity* (1961) to his 'sampler for student teachers' *Children's Writing* (1967), were just a few of the publications that developed this theme and set the tone.[2] As many of these titles were reprinted annually or biennially for at least the next seven or eight years, it is fair to assume that they reached a wide audience of teachers and students in training.

In 1958, Reeves had stated simply, though over-modestly,

> We attempt to teach children to write by making them write in prose. We should teach them to write verse. My years of teaching poetry were wasted because I did not realize this simple but revolutionary truth soon enough.[3]

Ten years later, after a flood of books and manuals on 'creative writing', and the publication of numerous enticing school poetry texts – Holbrook's *Iron, Honey, Gold*, Summerfield's *Voices,* Williams' *Dragonsteeth*, the *Touchstones* series of which I was co-author[4] – it must have seemed to some that the revolution in teaching poetry looked for by Reeves had been largely accomplished. Poetry – 'the supreme expression of the human spirit' – seemed to have achieved that centrality claimed for it by Reeves, Holbrook and a score of others. These included Ted Hughes, another practising poet, whose schools' radio series and subsequent highly influential book *Poetry in the Making*[5] sought to spur an audience of children aged beteen ten and fourteen to more purposeful efforts in their own writing. It urged them and their teachers not to aspire to a stylistic ideal or study 'How to write' but to tease out 'How to say what you really mean'. This, Hughes averred, is 'part of the search for self-knowledge and perhaps in one form or another, grace.'

'Grace' is perhaps a significant choice of word: the vocabulary and metaphor of the creative writing movement is often drawn from an amalgam of analysis and religion. It is no surprise to find HMI F. J. Godwin commending Clegg's *The Excitement of Writing*: 'When copies become generally available I shall use my heartiest endeavours to make it prescribed – almost devotional – reading among our teachers.'[6] The work of analysts such as Freud and Jung, psychologists such as Marjorie Hourd, philosophers such as Susanne Langer came together to provide new insights into the creative process and its relevance to the integration of the child's personality. There were too, in the application of such theory to classroom practice, echoes of Arnold's passionate espousal of a romantic, quasi-religious role for poetry – 'More and more mankind will discover we have to turn to poetry, to interpret life for us, to console us, to sustain us.'[7] The powerful moral and spiritual force of the Cambridge English school found common cause with the increasing emphasis on child-centred education, on personal growth and on the education of the emotions – all concepts that may be endowed with a mystical quality capable of being interpreted by those who, priest-like, 'see into the life of things'.

The writing of verse was seen as a means by which children might tap the inner springs of their own consciousness. They were encouraged to write 'freely', 'imaginatively', 'creatively', 'personally', 'vividly', 'intensely' . . . and did, as the many compilations of children's poetry show. The teacher's role was 'to feed the imagination, to stimulate, to encourage, to provide as springboard,' and the children's was 'to be spontaneous, to use their senses in accurate perception, to express feelings to respond to stimulus, to plunge into writing.'[8]

As the 'sixties progressed, other voices began to make themselves heard. Some of the approaches to poetry common at the time were variously presented as self-indulgent, undisciplined, romantically sentimental, overly concerned with psychic health, irrelevant to children's practical needs and thus tacitly elitist.

Teachers had seen something of this before. In 1927, H. A. Treble had castigated what he saw as the 'flabby superficiality' of much imaginative work in schools based on 'the expression of a miniature self that has nothing to express':

> Let the child express himself, we have argued, unfettered and unrestrained. Speech and writing shall interpret the innocent beauty of his imagination, his unconscious poetry, his ideals of life — forsooth — his natural art. So from a kind of illogical laziness of thought we have sunk deep into the slough of sentimentalism. [9]

Treble's angry concern about letter writing skills, spelling and 'language' being neglected is echoed half a century later by Stuart Froome in his 'Note of Dissent' appended to the Bullock Report of 1975. Froome deplores what he regards as an undeniable fall in standards of literacy and attributes it in large measure to the promotion of 'creativity' at the expense of basic skills.

> Sometimes work of very poor quality is displayed in such schools, because it is believed that the child's spontaneous effort is sacrosanct and to ask him to improve is to stifle his creativity . . . in the zeal for 'creativity' by teachers today, there is not the rigorous critical marking of spelling, punctuation and grammatical errors which there used to be. [10]

Despite the fact that the Bullock Committee as a whole dissociated itself from such views, there is no doubt that they were shared by a number of teachers. It seems possible that some of the high claims for the value of children's poetry may have bred resentment, possibly fear, certainly mistrust among those who did not share the perceptions of those making

them. Where such claims were clearly inflated and self-expression meant anarchy or licence because pupils' work was 'inspirational' and therefore sacred, a degree of scepticism was inevitable. In such circumstances it seems particularly likely that teachers had difficulty in perceiving what their role might be in achieving that 'difficult balance of freedom and authority' where children's writing of poetry was concerned. The words of a teacher in a comprehensive school interviewed in 1979:

> So, this sort of creative writing thing that came and went, I personally think it went a bit too far for a few years . . . It was creative writing and to hell with sentences, punctuation anything like that . . . I was in college about ten years ago — it really started then — the sort of thing where you had them all closing their eyes, sticking their hands in mucky oranges and eggs and writing about their experience — mainly the junior school thing. And half of them couldn't write and it sort of carried on to secondary schools which caused the old formal English course to be chopped . . . You look at the textbooks which have come out . . . [11]

The fundamental misunderstanding of progressive ideas revealed here is not uncommon but it is indicative of a genuine concern. The Romantic/Progressive school, failing to develop a broadly acceptable rationale for its work and failing to develop sufficient recognition for the discipline of art (particularly amongst teachers whose own experience of the arts in schools may have been severely limited) left the way open for a new initiative. Peter Doughty had put the case for a shift of emphasis very clearly in 1968. In what proved to be very much a forerunner of the kind of socio-linguistic criticism that underlies much of the Bullock Report's commentary on creative writing in general and on poetry in particular, he noted:

> The only kind of written work acceptable to many teachers at present is written work that is recognisable as one variety of the language of literature, that is, intensely autobiographic, densely metaphoric, syntactically highly informal and devoted to the accurate reporting of personal response to experience. From the point of view of the pupils' needs as a whole . . . the limitations of this assumption are immediately apparent . . . it ignores the nature and function of technical varieties of English, that is, the workaday language of a complex industrial society.[12]

The insights offered by linguistics and sociology into the relationship between language and learning and the social contexts in which learning takes place were a powerful new force in shaping the English curriculum. The publication of the Bullock Report appeared to mark official acceptance of a change of direction. The Report contained over 600 pages; three of them were devoted to poetry. Its stress was upon language development and upon language across the curriculum. Holbrook's work was, to his dismay, ignored and Leavis achieved the briefest of mentions. The work of the London Institute/Schools Council Project on the development of writing abilities[13] was very much in evidence and no mention was afforded the attempts by Witkin and Ross to establish a rationale for the arts in schools.[14]

The Bullock Committee were at pains to say that their survey indicated a good deal of time still being allocated to formal practice in English and that the replies they received 'did not reveal a picture of the decay of such work in the midst of a climate of unchecked creativity'. In fact it seems unlikely that, for the generality of English teachers, the reading and writing of poetry and other 'creative' activities were either as widespread in the secondary classroom as the progressive teachers had hoped or that Stuart Froome's fears were justified. The romantic element in progressive English teaching reacted fiercely to what it perceived as the mechanistic aspects of Bullock. Poetry, self-evidently concerned with language as art and with expression of feeling, seemed of little importance in the new 'utilitarian approaches to language use and teaching' as they were characterised by Holbrook. Indeed it is difficult not to endorse Holbrook's contemptuous dismissal of the Report's few pages on poetry as 'apologetic and pathetic'[15] when faced with its inauspicious opening statement:

> It has to be acknowledged that poetry starts at a disadvantage. In the public view it is something odd, certainly outside the current of normal life; it is either numinous and therefore rarely to be invoked, or an object of comic derision.[16]

Of course, the Report does go on to claim some unspecified 'great educative power' for poetry but the gloom of that opening statement persists throughout the Committee's understandably adverse comments on the more outlandish approaches to stimulus/response writing to their final paragraph which states that poetry

> in many schools suffers from lack of commitment, understanding and the wrong kind of orientation; above all it lacks adequate resources.[17]

Literature in general and poetry in particular, so the message was received, were only one aspect of English studies and not necessarily pre-eminent. It is hardly surprising that this should have been so. Perhaps too much had been claimed by the progressive movement;

there were social, economic and political pressures for 'standards' which were, it seemed self-evidently related to 'basics'. The progressivism of the 'fifties and 'sixties was essentially soft edged and without a clear cut rationale that promised results. The new language-led revolution seemed to have a harder edge, a greater 'relevance' to teachers' and pupils' immediate needs. With the spread of comprehensive schools the literary culture that had been the stock in trade of the old grammar schools had begun to look increasingly threadbare and irrelevant in its traditional formulations based on a concern for the acquisition of cultural capital. Whose culture? What purposes were served in acquiring it? Whose interests?

In this context it is perhaps useful to look at Fred Inglis' survey in *The Englishness of English Teaching* (1969) which refers in part to poetry but ranges across many other concerns. It is worth quoting one paragraph, at the heart of Inglis' argument and central to the whole book:

> But the product of our schools, the individuals of our society, do not know what to do when they are faced with a poem, and consequently they have no way of describing or even of perceiving the significance of poems and poetry. I do not mean . . . that they dislike poetry unconditionally. Some do. The point is not important. What matters is that nobody has begun to provide an adequate language in which they can discuss a poem. They, and their teachers perhaps, do not see the poet as an image-maker, an iconographer nor do they know what images, of nobility, fitness, ceremony, courtesy, they lack.[18]

The echoes of Arnold, Leavis and Lawrence are unmistakable. Underpinning such a comment is a moral judgement upon the spiritual barrenness of the age, something akin to the passionate anger expressed by Lawrence in his *What Have They Done to You?*:

> Your instincts gone, your intuition gone,
>   your passions dead
> Oh carcass with a board-school mind and
>   a ha' penny newspaper intelligence.[19]

Inglis' concern was undoubtedly shared by a number of teachers, particularly those strongly influenced by the Cambridge English school. Their selected 'high status' knowledge, mediated through and interpreted by them for the benefit of those who could discriminate, was not always valued so highly by a broader spectrum of pupils. As Bourdieu remarks: 'Teachers assume they already share a common language and a set of values with their pupils, but this is only so when the system is dealing with its heirs.'[20]

Inglis' research, was undertaken in grammar and secondary modern schools during the 'sixties and the response, even then, of what might be presumed to be the heirs apparent, the grammar school pupils, was a disappointment to him. It seems likely that Inglis is right when he suggests that nobody has begun to provide an adequate language in which pupils and teachers can discuss a poem but his appeal to images of nobility, fineness, ceremony and courtesy seems unlikely to be taken up. To be sure a language is needed but perhaps it should be one which does not assume mysticism as a prerequisite, one that children and teachers can speak with confidence. This is not to deny the existence of the elements Inglis sees as central, simply to suggest that they may not provide a particularly helpful starting point for the great majority of teachers and learners.

One cannot help but be struck by the passion and eloquence of so many who have written about poetry in schools. Often they are practising poets writing out of deep personal intuition, experience and understanding of poetry, offering valuable insights and generalisations from their work with young people. Gifted and inspirational teachers themselves, they have given much to many teachers but, paradoxically, it may be that this very commitment to their art sometimes distances it for less passionate souls daunted by meeting such high aspirations with 3B on a wet Thursday morning. Poetry may be held as being in some sense sacred, 'a constant reminder of all that is ineffable', as Holbrook remarks, but representing it in this way implies that it is open only to the initiate and may erect a considerable barrier to those who do not see poetry as necessarily providing access to some metaphysical truth. To remain accessible it is perhaps important for poetry to be in some sense anything but sacred. We might do well to remember Auden and Garrett's Introduction to *The Poet's Tongue*[21] where, having chided those who see poetry as 'uplift', they remark: 'A great many people dislike the idea of poetry as they dislike over-earnest people, because they imagine it is always worrying about the eternal verities. Those, in Mr Spender's words, who try to put poetry on a pedestal only succeed in putting it on the shelf.'

Encouraging pupils to write their own poetry was, of course, one way of attempting to keep poetry off the shelf and of giving it back to the child. The work of so many writers over the past thirty years has amply demonstrated the importance and value of such an approach but, nonetheless, as one visits schools and talks to teachers and students, it is clear that something is amiss.

If I have tended to concentrate on the writing of poetry it is because to a large extent that is where the emphasis lay. This was, and still seems to be, particularly true of teachers working with classes in the earlier years of the secondary school. The reading of poetry seems often to be undertaken with the main, if not the sole intention of using it as a stimulus to the pupils' own creative endeavour. As the pupils

progress up the school the requirement to write 'creatively' generally appears to be less common. Here is one teacher's response to a question about the frequency with which he asks classes to write poetry:

> In the third year quite a lot, in the fourth year not quite so much and by the fifth year it's usually a choice. I honestly find it's not worth it. It seems to create so much unhappiness and distress if it's a compulsory exercise. I find quite often absolutely nothing comes out of it and sometimes when it does it's so bad it would have been better not to have done it.[22]

Another teacher goes further and not only discards the writing but also the reading of poetry:

> I find second years are much more amenable to poetry than the fourth year. I don't think we've looked at a poem all year. In fact I don't think we've read one . . . As I say, poetry in the fourth year is something I don't do . . .[23]

Perhaps she is right to avoid something with which she and her pupils are so clearly unhappy. Over twenty-five years ago Michael Baldwin stated bluntly:

> The more educated members of the community, the educators, have manifestly been inadequately educated, and yet the system insists that they pass on this inadequacy. Far better stop teaching altogether than to teach the painful painfully.[24]

It is not a new idea after all: L. A. G. Strong had complained in 1946 that it was because poetry has been mistaught and mishandled by teachers unfit to deal with it that we as a nation, fail to get pleasure from the art in which our literature is richest.[25]

In terms of responding to poetry rather than writing one's own, the traditional 'comprehension' exercise based on the reading of poetry still appears and tends to be used more frequently as external examinations draw closer. Higher up the school elements of practical criticism are introduced but there may be a strong reliance on notes which, if not dictated by the teacher, tend to reflect the teacher's views. Thousands of school texts with near identical annotations bear witness to such teacher domination of individual response. Some CSE examining boards, anxious to be perceived as being in no way inferior to 'O' level, may also set papers that force techniques of analysis and practical criticism on the pupil at too early a stage. Unable to give pupils the means to make poems their own, and sometimes never having possessed them themselves, teachers not uncommonly fall back on the strategy of listing the points that would gain the necessary number of standardised ticks in the examination. However much the examination boards protest they value individual response, the generality of teachers will understandably be tempted to play safe.

Schools and examinations are geared to 'product'. A teacher reading a poem may well feel that something is missing if no written work either 'creative' or critical is forthcoming. And poems are short: there is a long gap to fill after the initial reading – a gap generally filled by writing of one kind or another and by teacher's explication. Talking to teachers, one becomes aware that many are uncomfortably aware that somehow they are missing the point of the exercise. Mike Benton sums the situation up thus: 'worry about rightness, both of the poem's meaning and of our teaching methods, predominates and the worry is conveyed to the children so that the classroom ambience of poetry becomes one of anxiety at a difficult problem with hidden rules rather than one of enjoyment of a well-wrought object.'[26] This problem may well be intensified with the pressure of external examination. Yarlott and Harpin's survey *1,000 Responses to English Literature* indicated that only one boy in every eleven and one girl in every seven O-level candidates expressed any desire to read poetry after leaving school and noted that most pupils 'detested' detailed study of poems.[27]

It is possible to see both sets of problems, over 'creative writing' and over textual analysis, as highlighting a major failure in the teaching of poetry: the failure to develop strategies for engaging pupils with the poem itself, a failure to provide for and to value the individual's encounter with the poem or to open up means whereby an honest articulation of response can take place. In different ways both 'creative writing' and textual analysis may be used as means of avoiding this central issue. They *can*, of course, both be immensely valuable means of aiding pupils' understanding and insight but they can equally serve the purpose of providing hard evidence that poetry has been 'done': this is not necessarily to say that it has been experienced. 'Springboards' to writing are fine but they may allow one to jump further away from the poem: the observing, comparing, classifying techniques of some practical criticism may, as Peter Abbs points out, induce set patterns of response which 'more often than not, have excluded both the poet's creativity and the reader's.'[28]

At all levels of the secondary school then, though increasingly as pupils progress from their first year towards public examinations, there appears to be evidence of considerable unease over the teaching of poetry. Despite this concern, there is little hard evidence as to what the generality of teachers think, feel, and do about poetry teaching. Yarlott and Harpin's work[29] was confined to examination classes and did not focus specifically on poetry; moreover it belonged to the early 1970s rather than the 'eighties'. Doughty's valuable *Teaching Poetry*[30] dates back to 1966 since which time schools have undergone much change. Nonetheless, his complaints about the orthodox view of English poetry as a cultural heritage existing solely to be plundered and analysed for the right 'hidden meanings', his plea for the dropping of the timetabled weekly lesson, and his stress on the vital role of talk, not necessarily teacher talk, are all highly relevant to the concerns of teachers two decades later. Most other writers, apart from A. J. Oakley[31] to whom I am much indebted, have tended not to examine too closely what actually happens in classrooms or, when they do so, to concentrate on pupils' own creative work rather than on their response to poetry they have read.

One relatively recent and highly significant source of information on pupils' attitudes, if not their response, is the APU *Secondary Survey report No. 1, Language Performance in Schools.*[32] The very full description of fifteen year old pupils' attitudes to poetry reading confirms only too clearly the dislike of poetry that can develop during the secondary years. If one were doubtful about the scale of the problem a comparison between the responses to one of the statements which appeared in both the 1979 Primary Survey of eleven year olds and in the Secondary Survey of fifteen year olds dispels any uncertainty:

STATEMENT		*Total*		*Boys*		*Girls*	
		% Yes	% No	% Yes	% No	% Yes	% No
I like reading poems	11 yr olds	59.5	36.9	50.0	46.0	68.8	27.9
	15 yr olds	32.4	67.0	23.6	75.4	41.5	58.3

The pupils were not slow to point out the reasons for this growing dislike. They saw poetry as a compulsory school activity which was totally irrelevant to their lives and which was moreover something presented as highly complex and very demanding. Where any liking was expressed it tended to be for poems that were humorous, simple, accessible, modern, rhymed and short. The authors of the Report conclude:

> The reason for their generally negative attitudes seemed to stem from the types of poetry read at school and from the difficulty experienced in the process of 'understanding' it. Noticeable in pupils' responses was an emphasis on the crucial role of the teacher as mediator or translator. There was sparse evidence of pupils' experiencing poetry in terms of personal response.[33]

The Secondary Survey provided for the first time clear evidence of a massive rejection on the part of secondary pupils of much that goes on in the name of teaching poetry. It did not attempt to offer the teachers' perspective and this, it seemed to me, was essential if we were to come to a better understanding of the problem and perhaps change our practice.

CHAPTER TWO

What Teachers Say

Setting up the inquiry

It seemed that a useful ground-clearing exercise might be undertaken to establish a factual basis for discussing how teachers in the 'eighties approach poetry. To what extent were the problems expressed in the literature, in interviews with teachers and in my own early researches commonly experienced? What do teachers actually do with poetry in the classroom and are there any lessons to be drawn from a study of practice? The early researches included a number of taped interviews with English teachers and a very simple survey by questionnaire undertaken with a group of some sixty teachers drawn from a range of schools (primary, middle, secondary) in areas other than that intended for the main survey. The questionnaire consisted of open-ended sentence completions concerning the aims and value of reading, discussing and writing poetry and a similar question asking teachers to list any problems or worries associated with poetry in the classroom. Although only a sighting shot and not in any sense a rigorously controlled exercise, this preliminary survey proved invaluable in lending weight to some suspicions, modifying earlier perceptions and opening up new and sometimes unexpected areas for investigation. No great significance should be attached to these figures as relatively small numbers of teachers were involved – in this instance twenty-two primary, twelve middle and twenty-six secondary teachers. Nonetheless the range of problems and worries, all of which it is important to note were *volunteered*, was interesting:

Stated difficulty/worry	% Primary	Middle	Secondary
Finding suitable poems/lack of resources	27.0	8.4	15.3
Finding sufficient time	27.2	8.4	3.8
Lack of experience/knowledge on part of teacher	0.0	8.4	23.0
Embarrassment/inhibition on part of teacher	4.5	25.0	3.8
Imposing one's own ideas/being too dogmatic	4.5	0.0	7.7
Children's 'inbuilt distaste' for poetry	0.0	16.6	30.8
'Switching pupils off' poetry	0.0	8.3	19.2

Other problems volunteered by this same group included:

1 Pressure to produce a measurable end product
2 Personal lack of interest
3 'Tough guy attitudes' from boys who regard poetry as effeminate
4 Imposing one's own choice of poems
5 Own lack of proficiency at writing poetry
6 Differentiating poetry and prose for pupils
7 Pupils' insistence on writing bad *rhymed* verse
8 How to criticise helpfully and constructively
9 Stimulating creative efforts without being too rigid
10 Knowing how to follow up the reading of poems
11 Poetry anthologies too abstract for most children
12 Should one correct?
13 Encouraging children to write poems
14 Teachers' lack of confidence about/ knowledge of various poetic forms
15 Adoption of artificial 'poetic' style by children

and, mentioned by secondary school teachers only:

16 Inability to communicate own enthusiasm
17 How 'technical' or not to be
18 How to assess their written efforts
19 Pupils becoming inhibited as exams approach
20 Pupils shy and reluctant to discuss feelings
21 Giving shape and direction to examined poetry anthologies
22 Articulating pupils' response and keeping it whole
23 Can one teach poetry anyway?
24 Poetic expression is 'alien' and produces barriers
25 Promoting poetry with non-specialist teachers
26 Encouraging pupils to read aloud adequately.

Clearly some of the above, none of which was mentioned more than four times, could have been subsumed in the percentages given for the larger categories but, without an absolutely clear indication of the respondents' intentions, it was felt best to leave them as separate items.

To test how representative these views might be and to gain additional information, further small scale investigations by questionnaire were undertaken with primary and secondary teachers in other parts of the country. They volunteered similar problems in almost identical proportions. The only new addition, worrying perhaps in the assumptions behind it and repeated by several teachers, was the difficulty of 'finding poems that match the themes.'

There was no one overwhelming problem but perhaps the most significant point was the marked shift in the frequency with which particular difficulties were mentioned by teachers of pupils in different age groups. Thus, whilst (to my considerable surprise) 'finding suitable poetry' and 'lack of time' were mentioned most frequently by teachers of children up to eleven years of age, these came as a very poor second and third to the middle and secondary teachers' main problem of 'overcoming pupils' inbuilt distaste for poetry' which had not been mentioned by the earlier group. The related 'fear of switching pupils off poetry' and 'lack of experience/knowledge about teaching poetry' – also problems of teachers of the secondary age group – were not rated by teachers of younger pupils. It was interesting that 'lack of knowledge' (which it was felt could perhaps point to non-specialist teachers in a specialist environment) and 'embarrassment' should figure. Why be embarrassed? Perhaps the Bullock view of poetry as 'something odd, certainly outside the current of normal life', *pace* Holbrook, is indeed shared by a number of English teachers themselves?

Even bearing in mind the well-known limitations of questionnaires as a research tool, there did seem quite enough evidence of problems to justify a fuller investigation. Further discussion with teachers and student teachers confirmed this view and a much more comprehensive draft questionnaire was drawn up, piloted and subsequently modified. A final version was sent to the great majority of teachers of English and English within the Humanities in the eleven to sixteen range throughout a single County Education Authority.

At the same time a second line of inquiry was also opened up. Underlying a number of the worries volunteered by teachers – 'inhibitions', 'dogmatism', pupils' 'distaste', 'switching pupils off' – seemed to lie a fundamental breakdown in confidence brought about by a failing relationship between teacher and taught as pupils entered adolescence. It was felt that there was in some measure a problem of trust when faced with the kind of exposure of feelings which poetry sometimes requires – trust between pupils and teacher and between individual pupils and the pressures of a large peer group. The question of how pupils would respond to poetry when those pressures were reduced seemed worth further investigation.

Some work on small group discussion of poetry in self-directed groups had already been undertaken and it appeared to offer a way round some of the problems and inhibitions mentioned earlier. It seemed likely that asking pupils to work in such groups and studying tape transcripts of their exchanges might point a way towards a deeper understanding of how pupils of different ages come to poems and what they take from them. It was felt that this might well, as Barnes[1] and others had indicated, have implications for classroom practice. The comments of the APU with regard to the role of the teacher as mediator and translator and their feeling that there was sparse evidence of pupils experiencing poetry in terms of personal response were clearly relevant here. Accordingly, a programme of taping and transcribing pupils discussing poetry in small, teacherless groups was undertaken. Some thirty groups of eleven to sixteen year olds were taped. They were of varying composition with regard to size of group, ability, sex and social confidence. In some cases the same piece was used with different groups.

Attitudes and approaches to poetry in the secondary classroom

Responses to the questionnaire

The questionnaire was sent to teachers of English and of English within the Humanities in the eleven to sixteen age range throughout a County LEA. This included the great majority of such teachers employed by the Authority. In all, 175 staff from forty-three schools, comprehensive, upper and middle, responded, representing a return rate for the questionnaire of somewhat over 60%. Inevitably I was concerned about adding to the burdens of teachers and felt that the response of Lewis Carroll's Father William to persistent questions might be quite understandable. In the event I need not have worried. The care taken by teachers over answering the questions was impressive and many gave additional information; some even taking the trouble to send copies of pupils' work.

The questionnaire itself was devised with the aim of gathering specific information about

(a) the teachers' backgrounds in terms of age, experience etc.

(b) their experience of poetry through initial training, in-service work and reading which may have influenced their practice

(c) their approaches to poetry in the classroom – for example the duration and frequency of lessons or typical patterns of activity

(d) availability of resources and resources used

(e) material thought useful for various age groups

(f) their views on various issues related to the teaching of poetry, the value they set on it and the main problems they encountered.

Although a vast amount of information was made available to me regarding teachers' background, experience, qualifications, etc., it would be inappropriate to offer full details here. What was clear was that this group of 175 teachers represented a fair cross section of the English teaching force within the Authority and that their views, practice and problems may well echo those of very many of their colleagues elsewhere.

Initial training and in-service

Interviews with teachers had already suggested that initial training of teachers with regard to the teaching of poetry did not sufficiently meet their needs and that specific instruction on approaches to poetry teaching might have been rare. Although one must make some allowance for memory playing them false, only 43% of the respondents claimed to have received any specific instruction on poetry teaching in their initial training course. Although 70% of these teachers had found such instruction helpful, the remaining 30% recalled it as being in various degrees unhelpful. Those respondents with an honours degree and a PGCE were most outspoken in their criticisms of their initial training. Inadequate coverage of the topic was frequently mentioned: 'We had one seminar. It lasted sixty minutes,' and 'One morning session which I had no opportunity to put into practice soon after,' are two typical comments. Another theme is the irrelevance of what was offered: 'A one hour lecture by a man who clearly had no idea of the comprehension ability or interests of the child in the comprehensive school,' and 'Too academic/literary. Suited only to upper school examination classes – and *then* within limits,' would stand as representative comments here. These teachers had all been trained within the previous ten years and the one who wrote that no specific instruction on the teaching of poetry had been received was in the probationary year: 'It consisted of "if you don't like it yourself, avoid it." '

At the other extreme there are teachers who write of the enthusiasm even the 'inspirational' teaching of their tutors with regard to poetry, of 'possibilities opened up', limited perceptions 'changed and widened'. It is noticeable that most of the positive comments about initial training refer not to such personal experience of sharing poetry but to the seemingly more pressing practical techniques of presentation: 'It showed possible approaches, gave encouragement, demonstrated that results could be achieved, which is about all one can ask of a PGCE course.'

Reading through the comments, it is difficult to resist the suggestion that for many of these teachers in training there was an implied assumption on the part of their tutors that they had already acquired a knowledge, understanding of and liking for poetry and that "practical approaches" were all that they now needed. Nothing could be further from the truth as any conversation with students on initial training courses rapidly reveals. With relatively few exceptions, their knowledge of writers is limited to the standard line of approved poets set for public examinations. They read little beyond this for their own interest or pleasure and in not a few cases express a dislike of poetry which they will, *mirabile dictu*, trace back to their own experience in secondary school. And so the wheel comes full circle unless a positive effort is made at this stage.

There is little chance of rescuing the situation later; 86% of the teachers noted that they had not attended any course, conference or in-service training on the teaching of poetry within the past five years. Of the remaining 14% few had attended any meetings dealing specifically with poetry and when they had it was usually for an hour or two within the agenda of a larger course or conference. The need is great but, perhaps understandably, it is perceived to be greater in other areas of English work.

Teachers' reading about poetry

A third influence possibly shaping teachers' approach to poetry in the classroom is the literature about teaching poetry. Teachers were asked to indicate from a list of what seemed to be the main titles, which books they had read and which, if any, they felt had influenced them. Further titles could be added by individual teachers if desired. The responses revealed a striking lead for Ted Hughes' *Poetry in the Making*, with 46% having read it. This was followed by David Holbrook's *English for Maturity* (34%), Sandy Brownjohn's *Does It Have To Rhyme?* (23%), Alec Clegg's *The Excitement of Writing*, Holbrook's *The Secret*

Places, and Margaret Langdon's *Let the Children Write*, each of which had been read by 15%.[2]

As might have been expected these are, with one exception, books of the 1960s. The topic has not been at the forefront during the 'seventies and Sandy Brownjohn's book (1980), along with her second volume, *What Rhymes with Secret?*[3] is the first for some time to stir a popular interest in teachers of English. Perhaps significantly, her books are focused on techniques of poetry writing rather than upon reading and response and they are in large measure picking up where the 'sixties left off rather than introducing anything new. Their great (and growing) appeal to teachers is that they fill a clearly perceived need in providing a clear-cut and firm line of approach in an area where teachers know they desperately need guidance and example.

Every one of the books listed by the teachers was primarily concerned with the writing of poetry by children as though this were the main aim of reading poems. Whilst being the last to deny the very great importance of this aspect of children's encounters with poetry, I wonder if it might be that there was and is an undue concern for a 'product' from our poetry lessons. Some evidence that this might well be the case comes from the next set of responses.

The teachers' attitudes

Two open-ended sentence completion questions asked teachers to rate in importance (a) the reading and discussion of poetry and (b) the writing of poetry, in schools and to give their reasons. A third sentence completion question asked the teachers to note any problems or worries they associated with the teaching of poetry. All the comments that follow then were *volunteered* by the teachers themselves.

The reading and discussion of poetry

Not surprisingly only 3% of respondents rated the reading and discussion of poetry as anything less than 'important' offering between them some fifty-four distinct, though often closely related, reasons for this high regard. These reasons tended to cluster around six main points:

1 Its value with regard to developing children's awareness of the possibilities of language as in 'It sharpens their awareness of language'; 'It introduces children to new uses of language'; 'It can give greater insight into the infinite possibilities of language than can prose'. Almost half (49%) of the teachers volunteered such reasons, making this by far the most common response.

2 'Pleasure', 'fun' and 'enjoyment' of pupils were the next most frequently mentioned reasons and appeared in 31% of responses. When enjoyment was mentioned it was usually in emphatic terms (occasionally underlined or in capitals) as though asserting something that may be regarded as contentious, as in: 'Most of all, I think poetry should be shown to be fun — it's as simple as that. If this is the case in years 1 and 2 then poetry should continue to mean something important in the later years of secondary school. But it is absolutely vital that it is shown to be fun!'

3 The value of discussion of poetry in encouraging a variety of attitudes and ideas to be surfaced and shared was remarked by over 20% of the teachers, for example, 'It gives expression to feelings/ideas common to all people which need to be shared'.

4 Poetry as an integral part of pupils' cultural experience was remarked by 17% who felt that it 'ought' to be covered. 10% of respondents referred specifically to the pupils' cultural heritage in one way or another, for example, 'Poetry and verse are an integral part of English and English culture and so an informed acquaintance with them is essential to a proper social understanding'. This point was several times linked to an observation to the effect that 'many pupils would not read any poetry at all if not for that done in school' or 'possibly the aspect of literature they are least likely to approach of their own accord'.

5 Fifteen per cent of respondents mentioned the value of poetry in extending observation and understanding of 'the world' or 'life' and a similar percentage, often the same people, remarked its value in extending pupils' observation, experience and understanding of emotion or feelings. It 'can only make them more sensitive to themselves, others and all aspects of life and the world', and is seen variously as 'deepening spiritual feeling', 'awakening and fostering sensitivity', 'extending pupils' self-awareness' and engaging pupils with 'the form of expression closest of all to the deepest levels of human feeling and experience'.

6 Clearly such concerns as those listed above could be related in some measure to any literature. Poetry is perceived as being distinguished by its form and its intensity. Several teachers noted that it can offer examples of structured, controlled, condensed, disciplined writing which, by virtue of its relative shortness provided an important aesthetic experience which was, with care, accessible, susceptible to immediate examination and called for spontaneous response: 'Poems are short, concise, literary experiences, . . . short enough to be read in a few minutes, yet strong enough to support a towering edifice of discussion, drama and written work. The exact opposite of a class novel in fact.'

Altogether one has the impression that Matthew Arnold would not be greatly displeased by these responses. What has sometimes been termed the Romantic/Progressive approach shines through many of the responses. The line traceable from Arnold through to the Progressives of the 1950s and 'sixties is clearly detectable.

This percentage approach to what is, after all, a very delicate area of investigation is useful in pointing to the broad range of teachers' concerns but loses the individual voice. One viewpoint which clearly reflected many teachers' ideals and is implicit in many answers to this question: 'Poetry is about sensitivity to life. A poem is someone's direct reaction to experience – we are enabled to share the experience and the feelings it generated. I feel very strongly that a major aspect of my role as a teacher of English is to foster feelings of awareness, sympathy, tolerance and understanding and I find poetry helpful in this respect. And because poetry is important to me and has given me much pleasure. I'd like to share that.' Matthew Arnold would certainly have approved.

The writing of poetry

A shift of opinion occurred when teachers were asked about the importance they attached to the writing of poetry. Where 47 % had rated reading and discussion of poetry as 'very important', only 32 % put the writing of poetry in this category and the percentage of those rating writing as 'not particularly important' rose to 18 % as against 3 % for reading.

The most frequent claim – for the value of poetry writing in encouraging 'self-expression' – was mentioned specifically by 34 % of respondents and was often coupled with the belief that it offered 'an outlet for feelings and emotions' (25 %). Both these were seen as self-evidently valuable and some respondents went no further. Others saw it as a unique opportunity for something more intense: 'This activity may release the most valuable means of self and world exploration they would ever encounter', wrote one.

There is a cluster of related beliefs difficult to tease out one from another. These would include the claim that children are not inhibited by poetry writing, indeed that it offers a kind of freedom they do not find so readily in prose or oral work. It is seen as having a unique value for the individual pupil not least because 'being allowed to write poetry is a sort of licence to be sensitive – and nobody is likely to pierce the 'soft underbelly' of the writer'. Another teacher agrees: 'they can express deep emotions in this form without becoming embarrassed. It is for some children the only way in which they

can relate hard-to-identify longings.' Certainly some teachers feel strongly that the normal rules are suspended, that their children may find it easier to express themselves in verse for 'children expect it as a form where more personal feelings are revealed'. Some value it as vouchsafing from time to time a more intimate understanding of their pupils: 'Poetry is *revealing*' states one, 'and a means whereby teacher glimpses the 'true person' behind it,' suggests another, 'in the same way that Drama allows unsuspected qualities to emerge'. The comparison is an interesting one in that the word that recurs throughout teachers' comments about writing poetry is 'freedom' and there is a strong sense that this freedom comes about in large measure because, as in Drama, the normal ground rules do not operate, that relationships between pupil and pupil, teacher, pupil and task can sometimes be allowed to be subtly different when writing poetry.

Another freedom, mentioned by nearly one in five teachers, is that children, particularly the less able, often find it easier to express themselves without what are seen as the 'constraints' of prose: 'It enables them to experiment with language in a different form and even the weaker pupils find it easier to respond in this way. When freed from the rigid structure of the essay form, when they have to remember rules of punctuation and of spelling, they seem more willing to express themselves,' writes one teacher. 'They find it almost more natural than writing prose', comments another, and continues: 'It reveals to me how children with so-called low ability are certainly not remedial when it comes to putting their feelings into form.'

Such freedom is often linked to the idea of 'experimentation with language' which is mentioned specifically by 15 % of respondents, most of whom saw poetry writing as offering a unique opportunity to manipulate words almost as a kind of game which has value (a) in increasing confidence in handling the written word and (b) in making pupils aware of the possibilities of language: 'They can experiment with form, or imitate the method of a poem that they've read. They can play with words, become familiar with them, without necessarily using them in the conventional adult way.' Twenty-two per cent of responses mention that writing poetry stimulates greater attention and care in the handling of language, requiring pupils to think more carefully and to focus more sharply on their choice and use of words. The freedom mentioned above is not intended to be anarchy and 22 % also mention specifically the discipline and control that poetry writing requires. 'It allows them', says one teacher, 'to develop a sense of shape that is not acquired through writing longer and, almost invariably, baggier prose pieces'.

The intention of introducing pupils to the poet's craft is commonly expressed: 'I do see it very much as an exercise in craft, in techniques . . . In the classroom I see poetry as a craft, perhaps a question of language, indeed poetry in the making.' Some teachers express delight at their pupils' achievements as writers, 21 % remarking specifically that children find writing poetry pleasurable, 14 % commenting that children find it singularly 'rewarding' or 'personally satisfying' to take up the challenge of working within the discipline of form. First hand experience of the poet's craft, it is suggested by 16 % of respondents, is valuable in that it furthers children's appreciation of the work of established writers and even helps them identify with other writers of verse.

Many teachers would strongly defend asking their pupils to write poetry but, as noted earlier, there is markedly less support for this activity than for reading and discussing poetry. A number of teachers are openly hostile to the practice. Running the main threads of the argument together one would arrive at a statement to the effect that 'children's natural antipathy to poetry, which they find alien, irrelevant and "posh", is strengthened by teachers who make too much of it by demanding a "creativity" which most pupils, particu-

larly the less able, are quite incapable of achieving and which at best is likely to result in a falsification of experience through stereotyped work scribbled down as an easy option'. This is a mirror image of the position taken up by those who urge the value of children's own writing of poetry. They, as we have seen, would typically argue that 'children's great love of poetry, which is a natural part of their social, emotional and linguistic development, is strengthened and sustained by teachers who actively stimulate the creative powers which lie within all, even (some would say *especially*) the least able and that through writing their own poems children may explore themselves and the world around them in a deeper, more disciplined and more personally rewarding way than anywhere else'. This is, of course, to caricature the position but not greatly so. If one contrasts comments such as 'They know they do it badly and resent it', or 'they hate/dislike it', or 'most of them regard it as a chore at which they are not particularly adept and most of them find it inhibits their enjoyment of reading and appreciating poetry', with the rosier, almost Romantic views expressed earlier, then the sense of there being a fundamental division over the worth of this aspect of poetry teaching is very strong.

The teachers' problems

The uncertainties and disagreements that began to surface as teachers commented on the writing of verse were multiplied many times in their responses to the next question which asked them to state their main worries or problems about teaching poetry generally. Taken in full, with all the fine distinctions retained, the 153 teachers who recorded such worries or problems volunteered a list of no less than ninety-four separate difficulties. It rapidly becomes clear that the kind of unanimity which characterised their response to the question about the value of reading and discussing poetry masks a huge area of doubt and uncertainty and several practical problems.

A number of further issues concerning the writing of poetry emerged. Even when fairly convinced of the value of pupils' own efforts as writers of poetry, teachers were often far from sure of the relationship that should exist between themselves and their pupils as, in some sense, creative artists. To what extent should teachers intervene by initiating the work, or by commenting, criticising or suggesting alterations? The Romantic/Progressive teacher here faces a dilemma: 'I feel that the whole point of writing poetry is that it is very individual and therefore if you try to suggest ideas to the pupil you are automatically reducing their individuality.' It is clear that if the teacher's main focus is on the unique creations of an individual mind and these are regarded as the central and sacrosanct concern, there is no way out of the dilemma and the teacher may feel constrained to accept any slack piece of original writing because it *is* in all its awful singularity, original and therefore sacred. The pupils' aims, intentions and abilities come into question and some teachers clearly feel uncomfortable about the status of children's work, the rationale behind it and what their own role should properly be. Such a rationale could be founded primarily on anything from a vague desire to let children 'play with words' to a concern to introduce them to a craft or, in some cases, to a form of therapy. Most teachers contrive an uneasy amalgam of all three and, as we have seen, have a concern for a number of other elements besides.

One teacher, uncomfortably aware of the difficulty, pointed to the shift of emphasis she found necessary to resolve the problem — a shift from writer to writing: '*I* see poetry — the writing of poetry that is — as an intensely personal issue most of the time, and I don't see why I should ask children to express that emotion. However, as a craft it is a different issue, and that does not worry me so much at all.' Taking the pupils' writing in this light frees

the teacher to comment, help and, where appropriate, make some judgement about the merits of the writing.

More than one teacher in five mentioned specifically the problem of pupils' 'distaste for', 'prejudice against', 'hostility towards' poetry; many more did so by implication mentioning, for example, 'the difficulty of gaining and maintaining interest in poetry', or that 'pupils see poetry as elitist' or as 'odd'. One teacher voices a common complaint: 'Inevitably, when the word poetry is mentioned, children always groan. It always happens. Generally after the lesson or whatever, the children will admit that they have enjoyed it but the initial response is always the same. Why?' The fact that it is an initial hostility and indeed almost a ritual response indicates perhaps, as more than one teacher has remarked, that it is defensive.

Who are defending themselves and against what? For a number of teachers it is quite clear that it occurs at a specific stage: 'the third year stage especially with boys whose adolescent inhibitions and self-consciousness inhibit response; because poetry is not seen to be part of their macho image, because of their awareness of their culture which forbids openly admitting sensitivity and emotional response.' There appears to be, in some teachers' experience, 'a suddenly acquired built-in resistance to the possibility of *enjoying* poetry' in older pupils which is interpreted as a defence against suspicion of softness or commitment: 'They don't like it. They sneer at it and think it's cissy. They want instant entertainment and many poems don't yield their secrets at once.' One teacher sees this as a specifically modern malaise and blames 'The inability/unwillingness of the contemporary child to feel, or to show he feels anything'. Such bitterness almost invariably emanates from teachers who valued poetry reading highly in their answers to the first question. There is sometimes a sense of personal hurt. The teacher last quoted above continues: 'Poetry is an invitation to *share* subjective feelings and the deep things of life: beauty, love, suffering etc. There is tremendous resistance to this now; in this essentially anti-romantic age where the sneer, not the smile, is *de rigueur*. What does that leave us with, but comic verse? (Satire, yes — but that's too difficult for them)'.

Teachers encountering a background of resistance for whatever reason (it is perhaps significantly described as 'soul-destroying' by one teacher) find it hard to elicit anything other than a negative reaction and difficult to legitimise the occasional positive response in the face of such hostility. There is a sense of having been ensnared by the rhetoric which characterised many of the fulsome replies to the earlier questions about the importance of poetry and a despair at never being able to live up to it. How it 'ought' to be is defined in essentially Arnoldian terms: how it actually is in practice may fall lamentably short of such ideals.

Teachers' concern finds expression in dozens of small, interrelated and overlapping worries, no one of which is paramount but which, taken together, indicate a collective sense of unease about much current practice. Respondents variously suggest that children often find the language, imagery and diction of poetry 'alien', that it belongs in any case to the 'posh', that they 'fear it' and 'come to expect difficulty', that it is seen as 'wet', that it is regarded as 'a waste of time'. There is a feeling, noted specifically by 15 %, that a major difficulty lies in finding poetry suitable for mixed ability classes whose reading and comprehension abilities may be as various as their levels of emotional maturity: 'To make it broad enough to satisfy several needs is to dilute it out of all value very often.'

One worry, referred to specifically by 8 % of respondents, was that in such class-taught situations they felt that they were often too dogmatic, imposing their own views, working the class to their own interpretations. One teacher remarked 'I know what I hope a particular class is going to get from a poem and tend to lead them towards my end rather than allowing them to explore the poem for themselves.' This is often a sign of insecurity rather than of confidence. As another teacher remarks: 'I put my own response on a poem and find it difficult to accept other views on the spur of the moment when discussing poems in class. Not having hard and fast answers to children's points about poems makes me lack confidence when teaching. *I* don't know all the answers!' As pupils move closer to public examinations the pressure to provide 'right' interpretations increases.

There was a concern that, although concentration on teacherly explication of meaning and technique provided a safer focus, personal response was neglected. Several teachers voiced their fear that they were allowing the poetry lesson to become a 'dissection' or 'another comprehension exercise'. Some could see no alternative to the sad observation by one teacher that 'One destroys poetry to some extent in helping children to understand', unless it was the 'guilt over reading poems and saying little or nothing about them', felt by another. 'It's so hard to *teach* without in-depth analysis of individual lines,' despairs one, 'Is it because I'm entrenched in this approach? — or are we kidding ourselves when we think there's an alternative?'

One alternative in common use is to ignore the poem itself and simply use it as a 'starting point' or 'springboard' into other concerns: 'I tend not to discuss the poem but to discuss the subject of the poem. I read poetry to a class mainly to put forward ideas on a subject.' Another teacher remarks 'a lurking sense of guilt that the poetry is *used* for its ideas and the follow-up work, rather than being examined for its craft and language'. This 'springboard' approach, like the 'creative writing' approach and even like the teacher-led 'explication' highlights a failure to develop strategies for engaging pupils themselves with the poem itself. Although all three approaches have their place, they can become strategies by which teachers contrive to avoid the central issue.

About a quarter of the respondents had no

discernible qualification in English — a somewhat smaller proportion than that found by the Bullock committee in 1975. There are, of course, many non-specialist English teachers who enjoy their teaching of poetry and possession of a qualification in the subject clearly does not entitle one to an automatic freedom from problems — indeed, it can present its own. Nonetheless, over a third (36%) of teachers with no qualification volunteered comments indicating that, in their estimation, this lack affected their teaching of poetry in some way. 'Poetry has a place and could probably be successful with a class of 11–12 year olds — if I were more knowledgeable myself', writes one teacher who does no poetry at all. 'I feel less competent about teaching poetry so concentrate on other aspects of the subject', says another. 'I'm not a trained English teacher therefore I don't get over-enthusiastic about poetry. I personally prefer twentieth-century literature e.g. Orwell, Hemingway, *Kes*, Stan Barstow,' states a third and adds, perhaps unsurprisingly, 'The kids usually feel the same way . . .' There are references to personal difficulties in understanding poetry and to a lack of knowledge both in terms of resources and techniques. Significantly, in another question, nearly 20% of all respondents agreed with the statement 'I don't know enough about poetry myself to feel confident when teaching it'; a further 17% were unsure. Forty-two per cent agreed that they 'find it difficult to know when and how to introduce technical terms'; a further 24% were not sure.

For not a few English teachers, qualified or not, it is rarely the lack of physical resources, though these are not perfect, which presents a problem. 'Inadequate resources' did not feature strongly (5%) as a main problem contrary to the Bullock Report claim that 'above all it [poetry] lacks adequate resources'. It is rather a lack of resources in terms of personal experience of poetry and personal sympathy towards it that are at the heart of the difficulty.

A frequent concern mentioned by respondents is a fear of 'switching pupils off poetry', of 'putting pupils off poetry for life'. These fears come from teachers of all backgrounds and are not peculiar to the non-specialists: one qualified teacher remarks that 'having been "put off" poetry for years by poor "academic" teaching, I should not inflict the same on my pupils'. There seems considerable evidence to suggest that, despite the rhetoric, despite the lip-service paid to the importance of poetry, very many teachers do find considerable problems in practice. Some display a misplaced reverence that causes them to place poetry on a pedestal. This seems to be the result either of their own academic experience, making them feel frustrated when their best efforts are rewarded with incomprehension, or of their lack of knowledge causing them to defer to the mythology that poetry belongs on a pedestal.

Classroom practice

Having looked in some detail at the value teachers claim to set on the reading and writing of poetry in schools, at their aims, their problems and their views as to how it is received by their pupils, the next step is to look at practice, at what happens in the classroom.

The 175 teachers in the survey taught a range of classes across the age and ability range — eighty-seven classes of eleven to twelve year olds, eighty-six aged twelve to thirteen, ninety aged thirteen to fourteen and eighty-nine each of fourteen to fifteen year olds and fifteen to sixteen year olds. Teachers were asked to give an estimate of the general level of ability of each of the classes they taught and to indicate whether they were mixed ability, streamed, etc. Although a highly subjective and therefore not particularly accurate method of gauging ability, it served to give sufficient indication that a full range of typical classes was included in the survey and to ensure that no one group was notably over- or under-represented.

Teachers were asked to estimate how often, on average, they had taught poetry to each year group in the course of the first two terms of the year (approximately twenty-six weeks). The expression 'taught poetry' was to be interpreted as any activity, of whatever duration involving either reading poetry, writing poetry, discussing poetry or writing about poetry. The responses indicate that in many classes very little is going on. If one takes one session per fortnight as being something like the minimum necessary to keep poetry anywhere near the centre of English teaching rather than a peripheral curiosity, then these figures must give rise to some concern. With classes aged eleven to twelve, 49% of teachers claim to teach poetry *once a month or less frequently*; with classes aged twelve to thirteen, 58% do so and, by the time the third year is reached, as many as 66% of teachers fall into this category. In the fourth and fifth years the figures fall back to 58% and 54% respectively. In many cases poetry teaching was very infrequent indeed as, for example, in the 14% of fourth year classes whose teachers estimated that they introduced poetry into their teaching 'less frequently' than once in eight weeks. Five sessions (at best) each year must be insufficient to build any real understanding of poetry or to develop any taste for it.

On the other side of the 'once per fortnight' line the pattern follows one already observed: a relatively high point (51%) with the eleven to twelve age group followed by a decline to a low point at years three and four (34% and 42%) and a slight recovery in year five. Again, one can perhaps see that the public examinations are doing something to halt the decline though at what cost it is hard to estimate.

Typically, poetry would appear to be arranged as a separate lesson of over thirty minutes. Relatively few teachers introduce poems on an *ad hoc* basis or appear to feel that much less than half an hour is appropriate. There is perhaps an 'all or nothing' approach implicit in the solid blocks of time allotted in this way by many teachers. It is not necessarily undesirable for these to be long sessions if, for example, some kind of workshop is taking place but, as we shall see, this would not be typical. Most of these lessons will be standard 'three-box' sessions — i.e. read, talk, write — and they can be a fairly gruelling business. Sixty-one per cent of poetry lessons with eleven to twelve year olds are in excess of thirty minutes, as are 68% of those with twelve to thirteen year olds, 73% with thirteen to fourteen year olds and 83% with both fourth and fifth year classes. More than a quarter of the poetry lessons with fifth years are in excess of fifty minutes.

It seems likely that secondary school teachers with their day divided into periods of fixed length, feel constrained to fill the lesson, whatever its length, with what is recognisably a 'poetry' content — reading, discussion, writing — irrespective of whether or not this is an appropriate treatment for the piece being introduced to the class. To some extent this is simply the result of a logistical problem: any teacher who has drawn thirty poetry books from stock, tottered along the corridor with them and given them out often to the accompaniment of ritualised groans, is going to 'teach' poetry all period come what may. As we have already seen, there often lurks a slight guilt feeling that simply to read pieces and enjoy them without what is recognisably 'work' — i.e. 'product' — is to avoid one's responsibility as a teacher.

The pattern that emerges is not one of 'little and often' but one of fairly large, infrequent chunks. One might question whether this is the best way to familiarise children with a wide range of poetry, to sustain their interest and nurture their enjoyment. What appears to be happening in many cases is the same 'compartmentalisation' of poetry that concerned Doughty in 1966 when he complained that 'the "poetry lesson" sterilizes poetry by shutting it off from all other situations where pupils use and respond to language'.[4] If the 'poetry lesson' means now a period of up to an hour four to five times a year then this danger would seem to have increased since Doughty voiced his concern over the regular timetabled lesson. In several cases teachers chose to compartmentalise poetry by not looking at any at all until the summer term – 'when I usually have a blitz on it,' remarked one. Several respondents acknowledged that they taught no poetry at all.

Of course, such limiting arrangements, though not uncommon, are not typical and, from the evidence provided by the question that asked teachers to recall and record details of any poetry they had taught in the preceding five days, it was clear that there were many lively and imaginative lessons going on which appeared to be enjoyed by teachers and pupils alike.

A breakdown of the details of 184 of these lessons indicates that nearly all (94%) included a poem read at the beginning or early on and 59% included two or more poems. The most commonly followed pattern was the 'three box' shape of Read/Class discussion/Write. In the first year, 47% of the lessons conformed to this pattern, as many as 67% in the second year and 50%, 47% and 41% in the subsequent three years. Small group discussion was relatively uncommon and occurred in between 5% and 9% of the lessons recorded but whole class discussion was much more common and might occur in up to 86% of poetry lessons in the fifth year.

Although there were undoubtedly some quite excellent sessions described in the above accounts, where the teacher's enthusiasm had been matched by the children's response, the overall figures might give us pause for reflection. Is the 'three box' lesson too dominant? Some children interviewed gave a very clear indication that they resented reading poems because they knew they were always going to be asked to write something similar themselves: the 'sting in the tail' approach to enjoyment. Is it not surprising to find so little group discussion in these 184 lessons?

The movement towards written critical appreciation rather than imaginative response is,

as one might expect, most marked in the fourth year. Specific written critical appreciation did not occur in lessons with first and second year classes, but it appears in 9% of the third year lessons and 42% and 41% of the fourth and fifth year lessons recorded by the teachers. The examinations begin to make themselves felt early in the fourth year and there is no doubt that they influence practice to a large extent. Almost every lesson with the fourth and fifth year groups was directly concerned with examination requirements – certainly over 90% of lessons recorded with the fifth year and much the same in year four. The following would not be unrepresentative:

Read *Pike* (Edmund Blunden), *Snake* (D. H. Lawrence), *Dulce et Decorum Est* (Owen) – discussed for fifty minutes. A 'taster' lesson to get my 'O' level literature class into the swing of using critical vocabulary techniques.

(Fourth year teacher)

It is certainly one way of approaching three fine poems but one might question the underlying intention. There is, quite clearly, an oppressive volume of teacher-directed notetaking, comparing, critical analysis, writing of model 'appreciations' and so forth during these two years. Whilst all these are perceived as serving the cause of the examination it seems unlikely that they are doing much to serve the cause of poetry.

As examinations assume a larger importance so, in these 184 lessons, the amount of 'creative' written work related to poetry decreases. In the first year some 57% of the lessons noted included a creative/imaginative piece of writing, in the second year this had risen to 77%. It falls to 53% in the third year, 36% and 16% in the fourth and fifth years respectively. The peak in the second year, it is suggested, may be the result of teachers feeling that pupils' early enthusiasm has not yet been overtaken by adolescent self-consciousness and that they know their classes well enough for them to ask them to write original work. The first and second years seem to be a particularly productive stage; a view which was confirmed in both written and interview comments by teachers.

* * *

The above analysis of 184 actual lessons given by the teachers over a five day period was supplemented by a series of questions related to teachers' own estimate of their practice in general. From the answers to these it was clear that the practice observable in the actual lessons reflected the teachers' general principles.

As pupils progress up the school they will generally find that poetry is increasingly taught in separate lessons dedicated specifically to it: 64% of teachers claim to do so either 'always' or 'often' in the fifth year though the figure is a perhaps surprisingly high 46% in the first year (fig. 1).

There is a steady increase in the proportion of teachers expecting a written response when teaching poetry: for example, where only 12% would 'always' ask for writing from pupils aged eleven to twelve, the corresponding figure has risen to 32% by the fifth year. Related written work is a very common expectation throughout and it would seem that by the time the fifth year is reached the vast majority of poetry lessons would tend to involve written work of some kind (fig. 2).

The nature of the written work changes markedly over the years. In the eleven to twelve age group it is at least 'often' the case for 42% of teachers that they ask their pupils to write a poem as their task; by the fifth year this percentage has shrunk to 12%. An imaginative prose response is 'often' called for by 26% of teachers of eleven to twelve year olds and by 14% of those teaching fifteen to sixteen year olds. A choice between the two is frequently though by no means always offered in all years.

Written critical analysis or response to poems is, perhaps surprisingly, 'sometimes' required by over 26% of teachers working with eleven to twelve year olds and the frequency with which it is asked for rises steadily with the years so that by the fifth year 58% of teachers would 'often' require it and the figure 'rarely' or 'never' doing so has shrunk from 73% to 11% (fig. 3).

As noted in the analysis of the 184 lessons, small group discussion of poems was not all that common and teachers' response to a question about their practice in general in this area was not particularly encouraging for those who feel small group work to be important. The responses (fig. 4) do prompt some questions. Is it really right that small group discussion of poems should be 'rarely' or 'never' opened up by almost half the teachers of first years and by a third of teachers in years two to five? And is there not something rather worrying about the fact that typically 35–40% of teachers opted for the rather safe reply 'sometimes' in response to this question? Given the considerable amount of support offered to the notion of small group discussion over the last twenty years, it is perhaps surprising to find it so little in evidence in this context.

As the pupil progresses up the school there is a predictable narrowing down of possible activities in order to concentrate on those that are deemed academically acceptable or that teachers feel confident about tackling with an older and perhaps less amenable group; it is a kind of 'putting away of childish things' perhaps. The increase in analysis and detachment is not, of course, limited solely to the teaching of poetry but it may well affect the pupils' perception of what it might have to offer. The responses to the question regarding the frequency with which teachers discussed poetic form and structure of poems (fig. 5) are perhaps a small indication of the trend, as is the fall in the frequency with which pupils are asked to write poems or to experiment with poetic forms. Certainly the performance of poetry through choral speaking — not all that common even in

Do you arrange poetry as a separate lesson with your classes ?

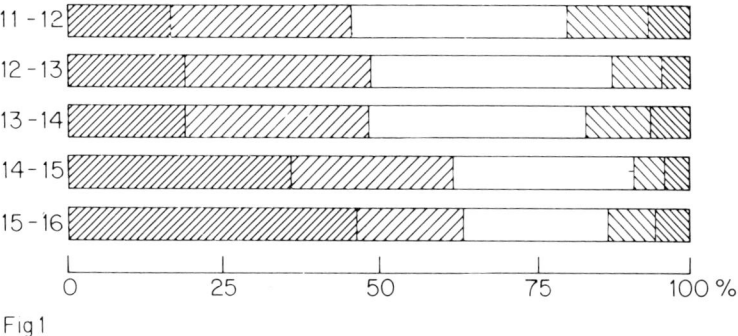

Fig 1

Do you ask for related written work when teaching poetry ?

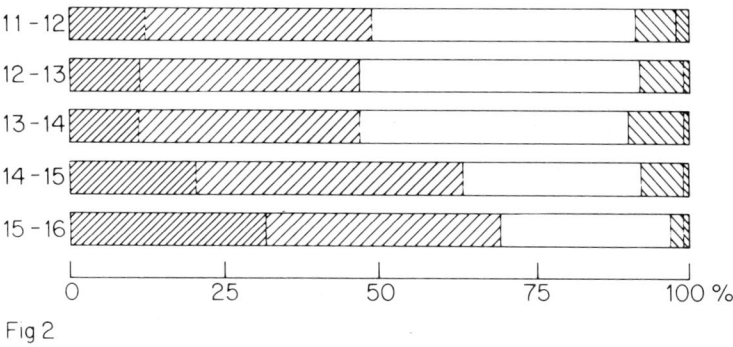

Fig 2

Do you ask pupils to write some kind of critical analysis / response to the poem ?

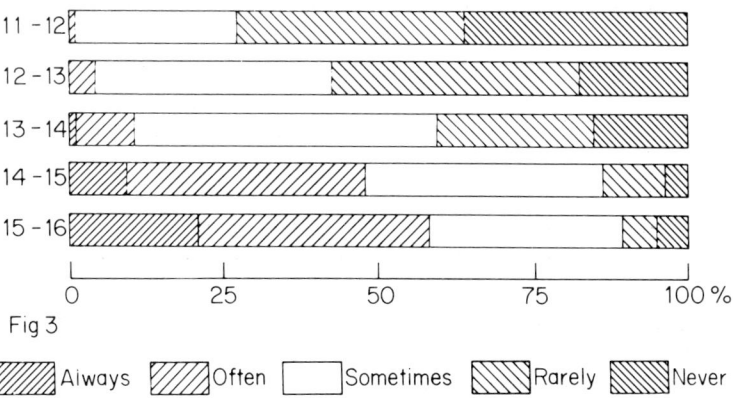

Fig 3

Do you ask pupils to discuss a poem in small groups after reading ?

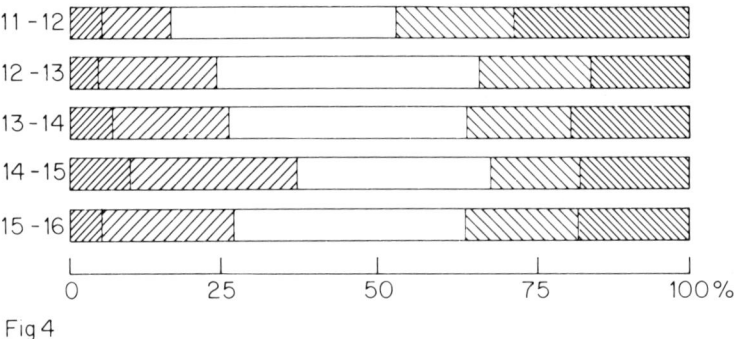

Fig 4

Do you discuss the poetic form and structure of poems ?

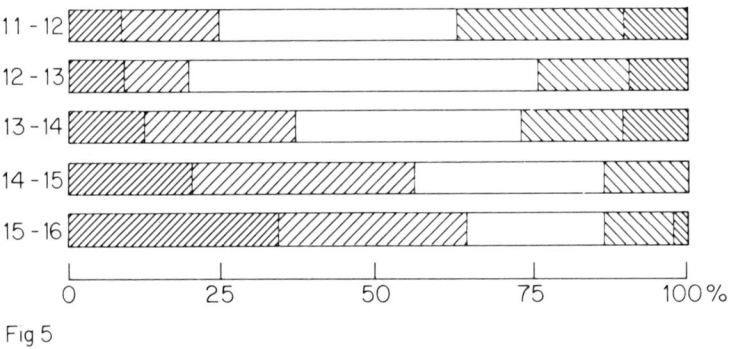

Fig 5

Do you use poetry for the purpose of choral speaking ?

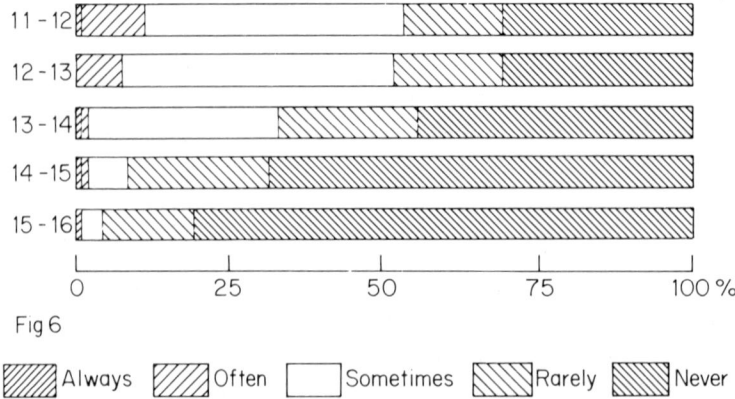

Fig 6

the early years – is seen as something to be left behind (fig. 6).

There is a steady decline in the frequency (never high) with which teachers work with pupils on class or group poems and with which teachers write alongside pupils or show their own work to classes. With regard to this last point, it is perhaps worth noting that 58% of respondents agreed that 'Teachers should write poetry themselves from time to time if they ask their pupils to do so' and that a number felt constrained to point to an inconsistency between their principle and their practice, offering reasons – time, discipline, mood etc. – which made it difficult to reconcile the two.

Higher up the school it becomes less common for pupils to show teachers their own poetry written in their own time (fig. 7). There is also a decrease in the 'publication' of children's work by their teachers (fig. 8). The movement is inescapably, some would say rightly, towards a greater degree of formality and abstraction.

The teachers' attitudes

The 175 teachers were asked to register the strength of their agreement or disagreement with a number of specific statements, all of which had originated from comments made by teachers in interviews before the project began. Some interesting patterns emerge as one 'reads off' trends through the five years of secondary schooling.

The enjoyment of poetry lessons by teachers falls off markedly from years one to four but recovers slightly in year five (fig. 9). Over 93% agree that they enjoy poetry lessons with the eleven to twelve year old group, 90% with the second year, 68% with the third year and 58% with the fourteen to fifteen year olds; by the fifth year the figure has moved up slightly to 64%. In the absence of information as to whether the enjoyment of teaching *per se* suffers such a falling off, it is not possible to be certain that these figures do not reflect a general trend.

Taken in conjunction with the many specific comments about pupils being increasingly hostile to poetry as they enter adolescence, it seems likely that the fall is largely indicative of a growing unhappiness stemming from such resistance.

Further evidence that many teachers sense a growing dislike for poetry comes from their responses to the statement 'Most pupils of this age group dislike poetry' (fig. 10). Where 89% disagree and only 3% agree with the statement as it applies to eleven to twelve year old pupils, the figures have changed to 46% and 30% by the time the fifth year is reached. Similarly, where first years are concerned, 94% disagree with the statement 'Teaching poetry to this age group puts them off rather than increases their enjoyment' and a mere 1% agree, by the fourth year 65% disagree 10% agree and the percentage of uncommitted teachers rises from 5% to 25%. Again there is a slight recovery from the downward trend by year five.

A similar steady decline followed by a slight recovery applies when teachers are asked to express an opinion on the statement 'Poetry is of greater interest to the girls than to the boys' in each age group (fig. 11). Where 74% disagree and 13% agree with regard to pupils aged eleven to twelve, by the fourth year the figures have changed to 53% and 31% respectively, though in the fifth year they have recovered somewhat to 59% and 24%. The same downward trend, though less marked, is echoed in responses to the statement that 'my pupils in this age group generally tend to regard poetry as "sissy"'. Where 7% of teachers agreed with the statement as it related to their eleven to twelve year old classes, 19% of teachers of fifteen to sixteen year olds agreed. The word 'pupils' in this question, of course, made no distinction between boys and girls. The idea that poetry is regarded as a feminine, possibly effeminate pursuit has some currency then and may support the suggestion made by a number of teachers that, around the fourth year stage in particular, any interest shown conflicts with the

Do pupils show you their own poems written voluntarily in their own leisure time ?

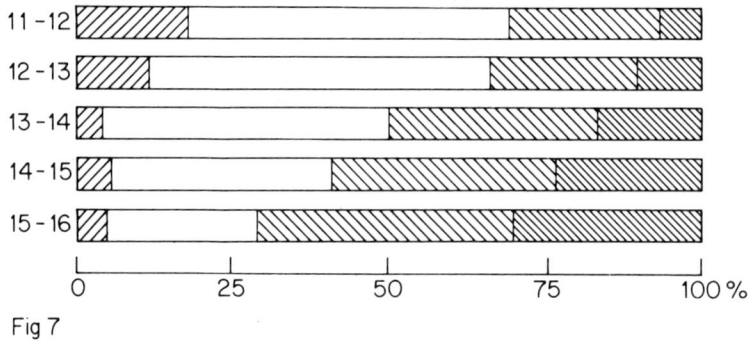

Fig 7

Do you 'publish' examples of pupils' own poetry either by wall display or by duplicating collections of their work ?

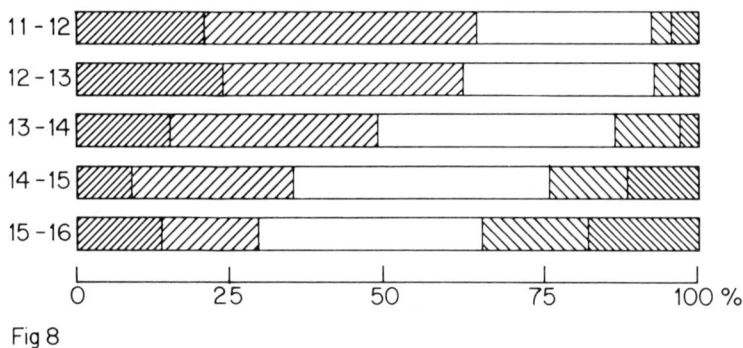

Fig 8

I usually enjoy poetry lessons with this group

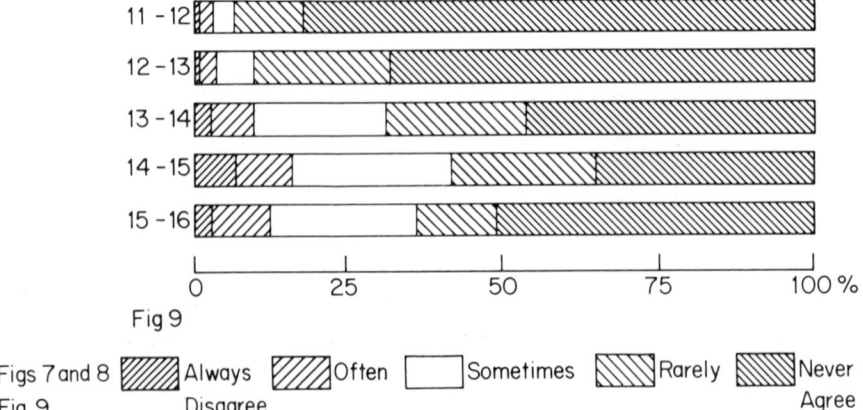

Fig 9

Figs 7 and 8   Always   Often   Sometimes   Rarely   Never

Fig 9   Disagree   Agree

Most pupils of this age group dislike poetry

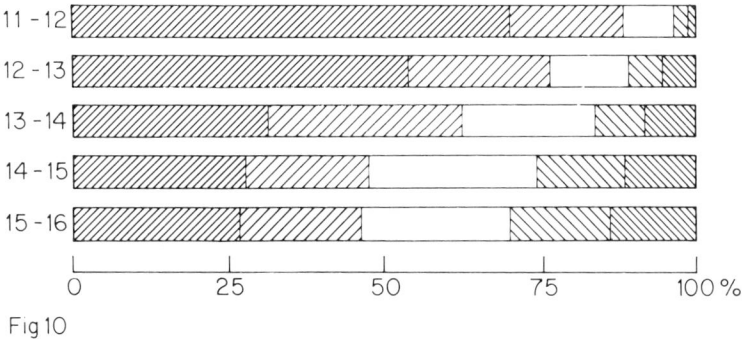

Fig 10

Poetry is of greater interest to the girls than to the boys in this group

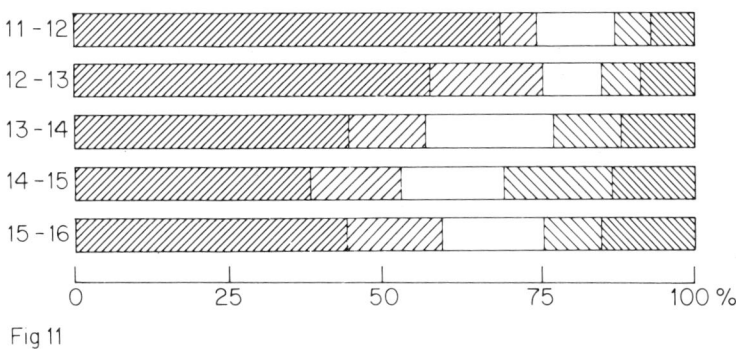

Fig 11

I find it difficult to interest pupils of this age in writing poetry

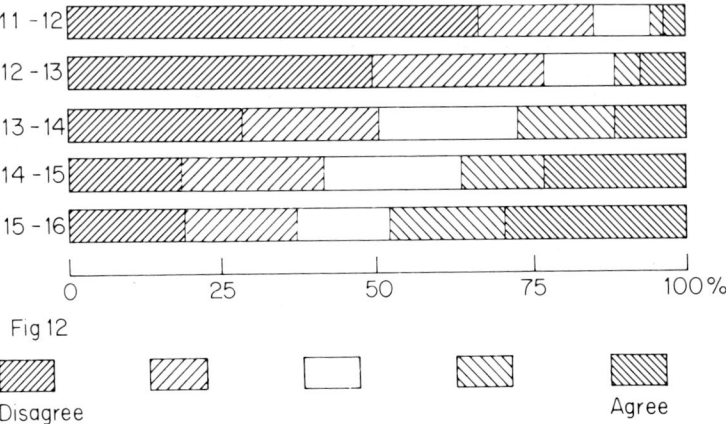

Fig 12

Disagree   Agree

adolescent boy's sense of what befits his male image.

Teachers' problems relating to the *writing* of poetry had bulked large in the sentence completion question reported earlier: the same difficulties are reflected in the responses to the statement 'I find it difficult to interest pupils of this age in writing poetry' (fig. 12). Where 85 % of teachers disagree with the statement as it applies to eleven to twelve year olds and only 6 % agree, the equivalent figures for teachers of pupils in the fifth year are 38 % and 48 %.

Several times the overall pattern seems to be that teachers detect a positive 'set' towards poetry in the first two years followed by a steady decline which bottoms out around the fourth year to be replaced by a very slightly more positive attitude during the fifth. Of course, this is a pattern which might well be replicated in terms of many aspects of school experience. Nonetheless, there does seem to be a general consensus that adolescence does make a number of pupils less receptive with regard to this specific area. There again does seem to be a suggestion that the imminence of examinations in the fifth year tends to help teachers by giving a none-too-popular subject a framework and an externally imposed *raison d'etre*, though even

Pupils of this age group often seem willing to express feelings in poetry that they do not readily express in other forms of writing

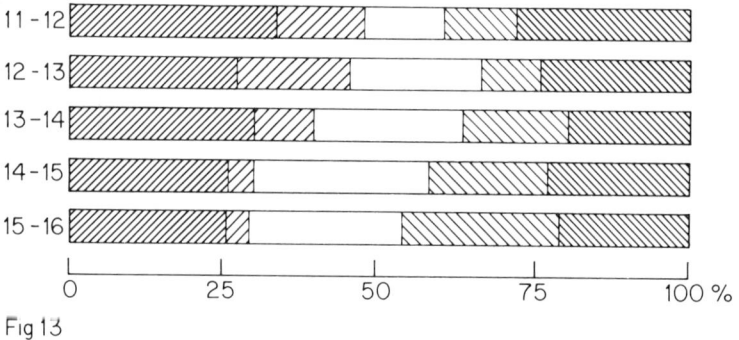

Fig 13

I do not feel as confident about teaching poetry to this age group as I do about teaching other aspects of English

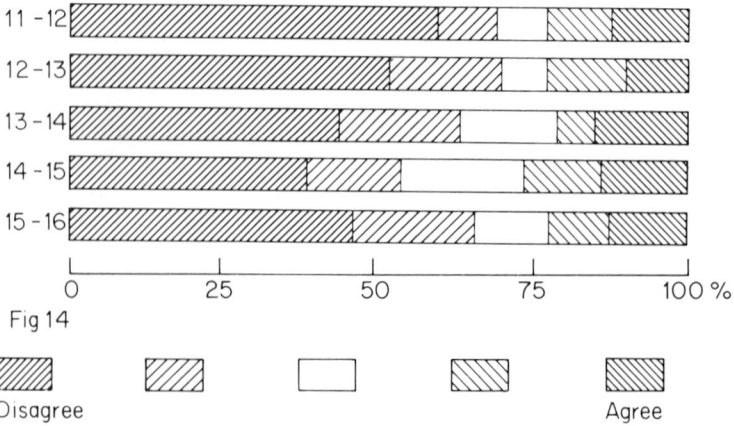

Fig 14

Disagree   Agree

that, as many of the responses to the open-ended questions show, brings its own range of difficulties.

The notion of a 'defensive' hostility which has previously been remarked and the implication that it acts as a cover for feelings may receive some support from the answers to two questions related to personal response. In one, teachers were asked to respond to the statement 'Pupils of this age group often seem willing to express feelings in poetry that they do not readily express in other forms of writing' (fig. 13). Some 48 % of teachers of eleven to twelve year olds disagreed with the statement and 40 % agreed: by the fifth year only 29 % disagreed and 46 % agreed. Whatever reservations teachers may have about the difficulty of persuading older pupils to write poems, there does seem to be a belief that poetry writing at this stage offers expression to feelings that otherwise may remain unexpressed. There seems to be a recognition that feeling 'goes underground' during adolescence and that writing poems may make it accessible. We should perhaps treat with caution assertions such as this one made by a teacher in the course of an interview:

> I think what happens is that, by the time they get to the third year adolescence is setting in and I do a load of poetry then before it takes over completely in the fourth year and they are all turned off.[5]

From the many responses that show the fourth year to be generally regarded as the least susceptible to poetry, it is clear that such a comment might, if perhaps tacitly, gain fairly wide assent. It seems possible however that there may be an undue reticence on the part of both pupils and teachers which stems from the pupils' defensive reaction. This, being overestimated by some teachers unwilling to take the risk of finding out, may deprive pupils of an area of experience which could be of particular value to them in mid-adolescence.

It may seem to be overstating the case to speak of 'risk' but, as is evident from their sentence completion responses, a considerable number do express a deeply felt personal concern. Not a few appear to lack confidence in dealing with poetry. Evidence of this may be found in the responses to the statement 'I do not feel as confident about teaching poetry to this age group as I do about other aspects of English' (fig. 14). The fact that about one quarter of teachers of each age group agreed with the statement does seem to support the view that there is a fair degree of anxiety connected with this aspect of English teaching; a view borne out by the fact that nearly 20 % also agreed with the statement 'I don't know enough about poetry myself to feel confident when teaching it'.

Resources for poetry teaching

It will be remembered that the Bullock committee remarked that poetry teaching 'above all . . . lacks adequate resources' though it did not go on to specify in any detail what 'adequate resources' might look like. The 175 teachers in the survey were questioned about resources and the picture that began to emerge is one that is easily recognisable in many other authorities and schools.

Although the problem of 'inadequate resources' for teaching poetry was not very often *volunteered* as a difficulty, a specific question as to how teachers rated provision produced a somewhat different picture. The LEA in question generally appears somewhere about the middle of most league tables for spending on resources, and the pattern of shortage that emerges seems to reflect as much on the disposition of available money within the individual school or English department as upon central provision. Presumably, were more money available, some of the low priority areas, class libraries for example, might receive a larger share. Textbooks, in the shape of anthologies etc., are seen as the highest priority with 80% of respondents regarding provision here as falling between 'adequate' and 'excellent'; nonetheless, provision for the remaining 20% was either 'inadequate' or even 'non-existent'. Over 35% of respondents were dissatisfied with school library provision of poetry books, 36% felt they were inadequately provided with single copies of poems and as many as 72% regarded provision of recorded material to be either inadequate or non-existent in their schools.

An increasing number of teachers are, of course, concerned about the common practice of duplicating poems in class and, as texts are expensive, they have been forced back upon the curiously nineteenth century method of writing poems on the blackboard to be copied down laboriously by hand into thirty exercise books. This seems an inefficient practice, likely to be damaging to pupils' enthusiasm and response though some might feel the practice has a certain Victorian value.

Perhaps of greatest concern is the lack of provision of single volumes of poems either in class libraries or as mixed sets of books available for teachers to draw upon as 'book boxes'. Room and timetabling arrangements in many secondary schools do not favour class library provision of any kind but it is disappointing to find that 83% of respondents replied that provision of poetry books in class libraries was either inadequate or non-existent. Children need to have poetry books to hand, to have the chance of browsing through a range of different writers' work, to see such books in an everyday context. The phrase 'children's literature' is almost always used to describe prose fiction for young people and poetry is forgotten: through the agency of the class library in particular a wider range of poetry for children might be brought to notice.

The class set of poetry anthologies is the staple of most poetry lessons in secondary schools. Teachers of eleven to twelve year old children listed ninety different titles as having been used in the two terms leading up to the survey. Such apparent variety is rather misleading as the field is strongly dominated by two series (*Voices* and *Touchstones*) which, between them, account for 50% of the 243 separate mentions. A similar pattern emerges for the other age groups. The anthology is the only medium through which most children (and very many teachers, one suspects) meet poetry. In many ways it performs a valuable service but, ideally, it needs to be supplemented by a wide range of individual poets' work. At a time when so many excellent volumes of poetry have been produced by poets writing with children in mind it is a pity if teachers are unaware of them and fail to make them readily available, choosing instead to rely on anthologies which, whatever their merits, cannot be an entirely adequate substitute for the single voices of poets as heard in their own collections; collections moreover with the merit of being free of all taint of the textbook. There are, it has to be said, several indications that many teachers are simply unaware of the wide range of poetry available.

Teachers were asked to give details of any single volumes of verse that had proved notably successful either in whole or in part. What is particularly striking is the ascendancy of Roger McGough and Michael Rosen in the age range eleven to fourteen. Of fifty-seven titles volunteered by teachers of the eleven to twelve age group twenty-one were by McGough and/or Rosen, twenty-three out of forty-six titles in year two and sixteen out of forty-nine in year three. No other writers were recommended nearly as frequently. The overall 'winner' across all five years eleven—sixteen was Roger McGough, whose various slim volumes gained seventy mentions (thirty-seven of these for *In The Glassroom*);[6] next came Mike Rosen with thirty-two mentions, Ted Hughes with twenty-nine, Brian Patten and Spike Milligan with fifteen and fourteen mentions respectively.

It was noticeable that the books most commonly recommended were without exception light or humorous verse: McGough's, Rosen's and Milligan's various collections, Eliot's *Practical Cats*,[7] Ted Hughes' *Meet My Folks*.[8] There is a clear indication that teachers feel they have discovered a workable seam here and that the sheer entertainment value of McGough, Rosen and others is seen as invaluable in encouraging a positive attitude to verse and in overcoming the hostility so often remarked.

Without in any way wishing to deny the important contribution made by Rosen and McGough, it does seem that a few teachers, having discovered an enjoyable way of discharging what they see as an obligation to introduce poetry to their classes, may sometimes be offering little other than verse of what Gerald Haigh characterises as the 'laid back' kind.[9] They could of course do worse and labour to interest children in poems in which they themselves take no pleasure: 'Far better stop teaching altogether than teach the painful painfully' remarked Michael Baldwin in *Poetry Without Tears*. Ideally, a variety of experience should be the aim but some teachers may feel it neither realistic nor desirable to attempt to maintain a balance between the different voices poetry can offer. It is worth remarking the underlying seriousness of much of Rosen and McGough's output and noting that children respond to their verse at many levels.

When one looks at details of single poems recommended by teachers as being particularly suitable for and successful with their classes, a similar picture emerges but there is not the same unassailable lead for McGough and Rosen. McGough's work in general, and some of his poems in particular, notably *First Day at School* and *The Lesson*, continue to be rated very highly and poems by Rosen are still frequently mentioned for pupils aged eleven to thirteen. Charles Causley's poems, largely because of the popularity claimed for *Timothy Winters* with the eleven to fourteen age group, receive forty-seven mentions, second only to McGough's

fifty-five. Poems by Hughes, Lawrence and Heaney are all frequently mentioned and not only in examination years. Some old friends – Carroll's *Jabberwocky* and de la Mare's *The Listeners* are commonly recommended; assorted Highwaymen still come 'riding – riding – riding, . . . up to the old inn-door' and some first year children are still enjoined to 'Watch the wall, my darling while the Gentlemen go by'.

Perhaps we should be glad of these survivals for varying degrees of pessimism seem to underlie nearly all of the poems most frequently recommended for the thirteen to sixteen age-group. The social deprivation of *Timothy Winters* – 'He sleeps on a sack on the kitchen floor/And they say there aren't boys like him any more'; the weary despair of *Last Lesson of the Afternoon* – 'Why should we beat our heads against the wall/Of each other? '; Porter's *Your Attention Please* – 'a nuclear rocket strike of/At least one thousand megatons/Has been launched by the enemy/Directly at out major cities'; above all, Owen's *Dulce et Decorum Est* – by far the most recommended poem, offer little comfort. Together they may seem to echo the grim closing lines of Edwin Brock's poem *5 Ways to Kill A Man*:

> These are, as I began, cumbersome
> ways to kill a man. Simpler, direct and
> much more neat is to see that he is
> living somewhere in the middle of the
> twentieth century, and leave him there.

It is almost as though the element of entertainment in securing the class's attention to poetry has been succeeded by shock tactics in the later years. Sometimes, as in McGough's manic poem, *The Lesson* ('A poem that raises the question: Should there be capital punishment in schools?') the two elements are combined to devastating effect. There is little room for tenderness or lyricism in these recommendations. Even the one highly recommended poem about the natural world, *Pike*, is about a single-minded, malevolent killer whose vicious jaws make it 'a life subdued to its instrument'; the one commonly mentioned poem about human passion, *The Ballad of Charlotte Dymond*, deals with a tragic murder.

Of course, there were many other poems (about 700) recommended, representing between them a very wide range of subjects, forms and treatments but throughout the lists recommended for thirteen to sixteen year olds there is a marked strain of pessimism. Not surprisingly, the general run of recommendations tends to reflect the range of material offered in the more commonly used anthologies. It is, however, important to remember that it is those poems that *teachers* perceive as being successful that are mentioned here. The 'teachable' poem is not necessarily the poem that touches an individual pupil's sensibility and it may well gain frequent mention because it raises a problem or offers plenty to discuss or to write about. It may be too that, to some extent, this choice of material represents a tacitly negotiated compromise between what is perceived as the pupils' defensive hostility towards poetry as effeminate and/or irrelevant and the teachers' desire to be seen as presenting something worthwhile that cannot be dismissed as 'soft'.

* * *

Many of the lessons of the survey are not new. What it does provide, I would venture to suggest, is some much needed firm evidence of what is actually happening, of difficulties that one had suspected but had not *known* were commonly shared. Indeed, it is often the case that, on presenting the findings to groups of teachers, there is a large measure of recognition and sometimes a noticeable easing of tension as individuals realise that they are not alone in their experience. What can we learn and what steps might we take to improve poetry teaching in secondary schools?

It is important to remind ourselves that,

although the teachers' responses reveal all kinds of problems and anxieties, there was still a very high value set on the teaching of poetry. Many teachers expressed their enjoyment of doing so and were convinced of the pleasure and benefit their classes derived from the reading, writing and discussion of poetry. The picture was emphatically not one of unmitigated gloom. The value of poetry in developing children's awareness of the possibilities of language, in offering a pleasurable experience, in increasing children's self-awareness and sensitivity, in offering another channel for self-expression and the beginnings of an understanding of the poet's craft were all, as we have seen, frequently mentioned by the teachers as were a score of other positive points.

Of the problems and anxieties, some can be tackled by individual teachers and departments as practical problems, some are as much to do with agencies such as training institutions and LEAs as with schools. Problems in both of these categories I have tried to indicate as the survey results unfolded: it is, for example, quite evident that in many cases poetry needs to be taught more often than it is, that there is perhaps too much stress on written responses, that there is a need for teachers to have a wider knowledge of what is available and so on. In the final analysis, however, everything turns on teachers' underlying approach to the teaching of poetry and, in the end, literature, in schools.

'If we know what we are doing when we teach poetry then we shall be secure; the rest of our work in English will follow by implication.' Holbrook may be right but I would suggest that this formulation and all that follows from it has manifestly done some damage to the cause. It is a rock on which to build a church but it is also a rock on which those with less faith have foundered. A considerable number of teachers are not at all sure what they are doing when they teach poetry and feel troubled that they do not share the certain security offered by an ultimately Arnoldian faith in its power. Others, whilst experiencing something of it themselves, cannot for the life of them see how to communicate it.

It is unreal to suppose that most of our teaching of poetry is aimed at the production of an elite corps of literary critics or of great writers. We are not, I think, in the business of offering poetry as either personal therapy or as spiritual refuge. Neither are we primarily handing down a tradition as a sacred trust nor yet offering the chance to acquire a personal capital stake in a national culture. This is not to deny that we and our pupils may find and take elements of all of these from our reading and experience of poetry, simply to suggest that if any of them, even subconsciously, is the main foundation upon which we build our teaching then it is likely to prove alien and irrelevant to many and will result in the further marginalisation of poetry.

I would suggest that there is a real need to focus less on the teaching of poetry and more on the experience of it. The Bullock Report remarked that the only thing poor readers had in common was that they did not realise that reading was something other people did for pleasure: something of the same seems to be true of the experience of poetry. If one could do a single thing to improve poetry teaching in schools it might well be to offer teachers the chance to get together regularly and enjoy poems being well read, performed and obviously enjoyed by others: it is, after all, an experience many seem never to have had. There would, it goes without saying, be no requirement to produce any written work afterwards.

This same delight in the activities of reading, talking, performing, needs to be passed on and to be encouraged throughout the secondary school years and strategies whereby this can be accomplished need to be developed — if necessary at the expense of some of the writing activities that take place. This is in no sense to deny the crucial importance of pupils writing

their own verse but such writing should perhaps be placed in a much richer context of reading and enjoyment of poetry than is commonly the case. There is perhaps too great a reliance upon the stimulus/response approach, and that at fairly infrequent intervals, for poetry to become part of the daily web of experience in English lessons.

The teachers' responses seem to suggest that we might focus more usefully on the poet's craft as it appears in texts read and pupils' own creative work. Perhaps we should have more concern for the actual writing, how it works and how it says what it seems to individuals to say. There is too much uncertainty stemming from the Romantic/Progressive assumption that creative work, whether the pupil's own production or the work of published authors, is sacrosanct.

There seem to be strong indications too that there is a real need to find strategies by which pupils can learn to read poems, to engage with them actively and to talk without teacher domination, without a nagging concern for 'rightness' and for product. Talk, it seems likely, is essential if we are to find ways in, to create the conditions for genuine engagement, and yet opportunities offered for talk seem very limited, for small group talk even more so.

It was suggested at the outset that there appeared to be grounds for believing that a fundamental breakdown of confidence and trust when faced with the kind of exposure of feelings that poetry requires was at the root of many of the problems. Monitoring pupils' self-directed small group discussion of poetry, it was felt, might offer an insight into the situation, perhaps at the same time lessening inhibition and providing the possibility of a more direct and personal engagement with poetry. Such a project was undertaken and it is to the outcomes of these small group discussions that we might now usefully turn our attention, bearing in mind throughout the patterns of response we have seen from the teachers.

CHAPTER THREE

'A New Effort of Attention': How Children Discuss Poetry

478	Nick	One thing about this poem is that it's a lot of effort to read it —
479	Graham	Yeah.
480	Tom	Yeah. Some poems.
481	Zoe	— On your own. It's not so much effort when you're doing it all together but on your own — to get right into it like we have done —
482	Graham	But in class —
483	Tom	— we wouldn't bother really looking.
484	Graham	You can't really say what you want to say if you've got a teacher in there, because the teacher's got their own ideas on it, hasn't he?
485	Tom	Exactly! Exactly! They don't really listen to us a lot.
486	Lucy	You can't analyse it just by first look — you have to go into it —
487	Tom	You've got to read it.
488	Zoe	You've got to go into it.
489	Tom	Yeah. They can put forward their ideas—say what they — say what they think about it, you know — but they should let us have a go as well. It's no good just saying — er — 'Do you agree with me?' You're bound to say 'Yes'.
490	Zoe	And you daren't say 'No'.
491	Tom	And normally you're asked to write a poem . . .

(Three boys, two girls: comprehensive school, half way through their third year)

Uncertainty and lack of confidence about presenting poetry, as we have seen from the survey, are not uncommon. The teachers in the secondary sector spoke and wrote with remarkable frankness of their problems, their fear of alienating pupils from poetry and of further developing what many regard as the adolescent's 'inbuilt distaste' for it. Many were concerned that, particularly with examination classes, they directed and dominated pupils' response to an unacceptable degree but felt they lacked the strategies to avoid this happening. It was with this particular problem in mind that the previously mentioned programme of tape-recording small groups of pupils discussing poems was undertaken. Small groups, working without the presence of a teacher might, it was felt, offer some insights into the ways in which pupils come to grips with a poem and the problems they encounter. To what extent might they echo the problems that the teachers themselves had noted? Might there be lessons to be learned about the ways in which poems are presented?

For the past fifteen years, the importance of pupil talk in the classroom has been strongly urged and it has frequently been suggested that the traditional teacher directed class, although it has its place, is not necessarily the only or the best way of engaging pupils' interest or of deepening their understanding.[1] With regard to the appreciation of a literary text, especially a poem, it seems that this may be particularly true. Poetry is often complex and singularly compressed, elusive and allusive, demanding time and mental space in which to feel towards an understanding and a sufficient sense of security to be tentative, to be 'wrong'.

The pupils in the transcript quoted at the head of this chapter themselves suggest that the traditional teacher directed response to a poem produces a closed system, a kind of sterile game in which teachers seek confirmation of their own interpretation rather than encouraging their pupils' personal search for meaning though they will probably still call it 'discussion'. The Bullock Report of 1975, commenting on the depressing research findings of Yarlott and Harpin in their 1972–73 survey,[2] remarks that antipathy to poetry 'rests substantially in the method of teaching it'.[3] The comments of these third year pupils would seem to add weight to the Bullock committee's unhappiness about the comprehension approach to poetry and the 'Procrustean bed' of the traditional poetry lesson where there is 'a temptation for the poem to be read, re-read, socratically worried, eviscerated for its figures of speech, even copied into exercise books'.[4]

These pupils had experienced nothing so deadening but it is clear that even they do not usually experience the Bullock ideal of joint exploration of the text, of feeling their response valued or developed in subtlety and complexity. 'Catechism or a one-way traffic in apodictic judgement'[5], despite the teacher's best efforts, may be the way in which the pupils perceive the traditional class poetry lesson:

600	Nick	. . we'd have about five minutes then the teacher would tell us what we're thinking about it.
601	Graham	But, yeah, the teacher would tell us –
602	Zoe	Try and tell us, try and tell us.
603	Graham	– what we should say this, this, this poem is on about . . .

Tom's comment earlier, 'and normally you're asked to write a poem,' with its accompanying murmur of recognition and assent, points to the problems of what we have seen to be another widely used and often unvarying approach – the 'three box' model. Here, a poem is read, a teacher-led discussion follows and, as this flags, the pupils are asked to write poems of their own on a similar theme thus neatly filling the timetabled slot, solving the question of what one actually does with poetry and going some way to making teachers feel they are honouring an obligation towards 'creative' work. The value of pupils writing their own poems is not here in question but when this 'three box' formula becomes the only context in which they experience poetry then the question of balance in their work, the extent of their engagement with what others write and the attention they give to it may legitimately be raised. All too often the effect is to move as quickly as possible away from, not further into, the poem which is thereby relegated to the status of 'stimulus' rather than being valued for and in itself.

The third years whose thoughts are transcribed above were tape recorded as an unsupervised group and their comments came towards the end of a lively conversation which lasted over 600 exchanges and some forty-five minutes. That in itself is worth remarking for, by their own account, even with a skilful and enlightened teacher, the group's engagement with the poem would probably have taken quite a different form:

464 · Graham   I'd just read it and let the teacher say what — I'd just sit there, read it and let the teacher say what they wanted to and not really think about it.

465   Tom   Yeah.

466   Nick   Whatever we say, they're going to say something and if it's totally different — well — and they nat — and we naturally assume that we're wrong.

The poem under discussion was *The Warm and the Cold* by Ted Hughes[6]. Experience with other groups supported the findings reported in *Schools Council Working Paper 64*[7] that the structure for group activity in the form of instructions or questions 'should offer the children a secure framework but should not be so restrictive that any form of exploratory thinking is curtailed' and, after hearing the poem read aloud, the group was given a general instruction. This was to talk about the poem in any way they pleased but at some point to consider (i) what the poem was about (ii) how it said what it was saying (iii) any things they liked or disliked about it (iv) why they felt as they did about it. It was made clear that these were not tasks to be taken in order and that they could organise the discussion in any way they chose. The group was left unsupervised in a small room close to but uninterrupted by the rest of the class. No time limit was given. The

whole of the conversation is too long to reproduce here but various key stages and elements in its development are worth noting. First the opening exchanges:

1   Graham   You read it through again, you're the brainy one.

2   Nick   Oh, thanks . . . Do you want me to do it verse by verse?

3   Tom   Oh yeah, I suppose so.

4   Nick   (Reads verse 1 aloud)

5   Tom   What does this bit 'a butterfly in its mummy' mean?

6   Graham   Pupa.

7   Zoe   Pupa.

8   Tom   Aah!

9   Graham   Tucked up 'like a viol in its case.'

10   Tom   Yeah.

11   Graham   In other words . . . it's shut in.

12   Nick   And what he's saying is everything's got a place to go.

13   Tom   Sort of like a snug fit.

14   Zoe   Yes.

15   Tom   Aah!

16   Nick   It's getting cold outside but everybody —

17   Zoe   — Is warm.

Working in this way was a new experience for the pupils. It is interesting that when the responsibility falls to them their first instinct is to give one of their number a teacherly role. From the security of that arrangement they begin, gingerly, to move further in, re-reading the poem, re-telling it, rehearsing individual lines. They concentrate from the outset very largely on the specific meanings of words or single images — '**What does this bit mean?**' — yet early on they have an intuitive feeling for the central concerns of the poem even though particular meanings escape them. There seems to be a need to realise the poem in concrete terms. Graham's 'Tucked up' (line 9) is an interpolation building on the earlier line of the poem 'And the badger in its bedding' which

The Warm and the Cold

Freezing dusk is closing
  Like a slow trap of steel
On trees and roads and hills and all
  That can no longer feel.
    But the carp is in its depth
      Like a planet in its heaven.
    And the badger in its bedding
      Like a loaf in the oven.
    And the butterfly in its mummy
      Like a viol in its case.
    And the owl in its feathers
      Like a doll in its lace.

Freezing dusk has tightened
  Like a nut screwed tight
On the starry aeroplane
  Of the soaring night.
    But the trout is in its hole
      Like a chuckle in a sleeper.
    The hare strays down the highway
      Like a root going deeper.
    The snail is dry in the outhouse
      Like a seed in a sunflower.
    The owl is pale on the gatepost
      Like a clock on its tower.

Moonlight freezes the shaggy world
  Like a mammoth of ice—
The past and the future
  Are the jaws of a steel vice.
    But the cod is in the tide-rip
      Like a key in a purse.
    The deer are on the bare-blown hill
      Like smiles on a nurse.
    The flies are behind the plaster
      Like the lost score of a jig.
    Sparrows are in the ivy-clump
      Like money in a pig.

Such a frost
  The flimsy moon
    Has lost her wits.

    A star falls.

The sweating farmers
  Turn in their sleep
    Like oxen on spits.

Ted Hughes

relates the 'mummy' image forward to that of the viol. Nick, who immediately had the mantle of surrogate teacher thrust upon him at the outset, is quick to generalise this insight to the whole poem: 'And what he's saying is everything's got a place to go' (line 12). Similarly, Tom's use of 'snug' at line 13 triggers the generalising comments at lines 16 and 17, 'It's getting cold outside but everybody/Is warm.'

The group does not continue this line of interpretative comment but returns to specific problems of meaning, subjecting the lines to what might almost be described as a light sampling.

18	*Graham*	'The carp is in its depth/Like a planet in its heaven.'
19	*Zoe*	What's a carp?
20	*Nick*	It's a fish.
21	*Graham*	It's a fish.
22	*Graham*	'Like a planet in its heaven . . .' – doesn't sound right.
23	*Tom*	What's 'a planet in its . . .' What's 'a planet in its heaven'?
24	*Nick*	Well, it's all got a place to be, hasn't it?
25	*Tom*	Yeah, I don't s . . .
26	*Graham*	'Planet in its heaven . . .'
27	*Tom*	I suppose it's just place, yeah, must be, yeah, yeah **Right**. **OK**. Second verse.

The repetition or re-telling of lines as at lines 18, 22 and 26 is a common feature of the early engagement with a poem. Individuals constantly try lines over, not always with a view to saying anything particular about them but often either to 'savour' them and/or to verbalise the problem they may pose – 'thinking aloud' as it were. There is an implicit recognition that meaning-making may require words to be read aloud and not heard only in the head. Here Graham's concern is essentially a puzzlement over the poetic use of the word 'heaven' which,

in this context, is unfamiliar to him. Over 500 exchanges later he returns to it and is able to explain more precisely why it 'doesn't sound right':

546	*Graham*	'A planet in its heaven . . .' – you wouldn't think of a planet's heaven, you'd think of a planet in its universe or its path or –
547	*Tom*	In its solar system, in its galaxy.

The chance to return and to ponder a line in this way would not generally present itself in a teacher directed lesson. On the other hand, only a teacher could supply the group with the information that they lack.

Explication – the literal 'unfolding' of the text – involves the sharing of information within the group and a willingness to declare uncertainty or puzzlement. Zoe, who so confidently supplies the word 'pupa' at line 7, is perhaps surprisingly nonplussed by a word that a teacher might have expected her to know: 'What's a carp?' she asks at line 19. It seems possible that such uncertainties are less likely to be recognised by the teacher or voiced by the pupil in whole-class discussion. Even quiet Lucy ventures a question in the next set of exchanges:

28	*Nick*	Your turn.
29	*Tom*	Oh . . . (*Reads verse 2 aloud*)
30	*Lucy*	What does 'a trout in its hole' mean?
31	*Tom*	A what?
32	*Lucy*	'Trout is in its hole . . .'
33	*Tom*	Where a trout sleeps.
34	*Lucy*	Oh.
35	*Graham*	Does it?
36	*Lucy*	I thought they were just suspended in the water.
37	*Tom*	No, it's got a little hole.
38	*Graham*	'a chuckle in a sleeper . . .' What's 'a chuckle in a sleeper'?

39	*Tom*	Oh, yes.
40	*Nick*	Well, a sleeper could be –
41	*Zoe*	A railway sleeper –
42	*Graham*	A railway sleeper, yeah. So a chuckle might be –
43	*Tom*	Yeah – or a sleeper can be a person sleeping.
44	*Graham*	Or a train . . . (*laughter*) . . . On a train . . .
45	*Tom*	I mean – erm –
46	*Zoe*	What's the chuckle bit then?

Again there is immediate concern for specific meaning, a need to 'place' the facts of the poem. Nonetheless, Zoe's question at line 46 is only partly answered and is lost in a further trying over of lines:

47	*Graham*	'The owl is pale on the gatepost . . .'
48	*Tom*	Yeah.
49	*Graham*	'Like a clock on its tower.'
50	*Zoe*	Do they sleep on gateposts?
51	*Tom*	Yeah, owls usually sleep on gateposts or something like that don't they?
52	*Nick*	They usually sleep in trees.
53	*Zoe*	They sleep on gateposts too.
54	*Tom*	They go hunting at night so they'd have a rest on the gatepost, wouldn't they?
55	*Nick*	Anyway, if you're asleep on a gatepost in the middle of the afternoon and you thought –
56	*Tom*	It's not the middle of the afternoon, is it?
57	*Zoe*	It makes it feel like dusk.
58	*Nick*	It's dusk.
59	*Tom*	It's dusk. Well, I mean . . .
60	*Zoe*	Late afternoon.
61	*Tom*	It's not the afternoon is it?
62	*Zoe*	Late afternoon.
63	*Tom*	Seven o'clock, isn't it?
64	*Graham*	Look: 'Freezing dusk has tightened/Like a nut screwed tight.' It's clever.

65	*Zoe*	It's getting darker and darker.
66	*Tom*	Yeah, yeah! (*excitedly*)

The need for clear visualisation of the images is once more marked though, at first sight, some of the exchanges may seem trivial. In fact a more significant exchange than might at first appear takes place between lines 54 and 58. Tom's observation that owls hunt at night is rather flippantly taken by Nick to imply that this particular owl is therefore asleep during the day (line 55). Tom corrects the inference and thus moves the discussion into what is a new phase by causing Zoe to voice her agreement of his interpretation, thus forcing Nick to look again at the text and reject his earlier reading and eventually leading Graham to refer to the text for confirmation and to make his involuntary value judgement at line 64: 'It's clever.' From this point on it is as though Tom's correction of Nick's earlier misunderstanding and Graham's evident pleasure in the line give the group the necessary impetus to treat the poem as being worthy of serious attention. They are 'learning to trust the poem and to feel it trustworthy'.[8] Zoe is the first to see that a process is at work in the poem, that it is not static in time (line 65); Tom excitedly supports her observation and Graham, caught almost unawares by the poem's 'cleverness', reads on without prompting. The degree of concentration is striking:

67	*Graham*	'Moonlight freezes the shaggy world
		        Like a mammoth of ice –
		The past and the future
		        Are the jaws of a steel vice.'

68	*Nick*	That's steel again.
69	*Tom*	Yeah.
70	*Nick*	It's the same type of simile.
71	*Tom*	Yeah, it's the cold –
72	*Zoe*	Yes. Hard –
73	*Nick*	It's got the steel vice and the steel trap at the top.

74	*Tom*	Yeah. It's a cold and hard job, yeah.
75	*Graham*	'But the cod is in the tide rip Like a key in a purse.'
76	*Nick*	It's the third fish!
77	*Tom*	Yeah . . . well . . .
78	*Graham*	Looks like fish . . . *(continues reading verse)*

Nick sees the pattern emerging (line 68) when he links the opening lines of the first and third verses (line 73) thus allowing Tom and Zoe to see the points of comparison and the appropriateness of the images (lines 71 and 72), characteristically summed up by Tom at line 74, though it takes until line 230 for the opening of verse two to be similarly related. As soon as Graham continues reading at line 75, Nick perceives the pattern – 'it's the third fish!' – thus alerting Tom and Graham to an idea that both take up later (lines 102–107). For the moment, the point is set aside. The group is engaged in a process described by James Britton as 'leapfrogging' and, throughout this and other tapes there is considerable evidence to support his view that

> a leapfrogging of listening and speaking may be in fact the characteristic feature of a joint exploration in talk and account for its value; each may give what he could not have given it had it not been for the 'taking' and in turn what he gives may provide someone else's starting point. [9]

Graham finishes reading the third verse and its unusual images at once create problems:

79	*Tom*	Well, I don't get that bit – 'The flies are behind the plaster/Like the lost score of a jig.' – What does that mean?
80	*Lucy*	No, . . . erm . . . no idea.
81	*Zoe*	It means they're frozen in.
82	*Graham*	(?) . . they'd plastered the window for the fire going.
83	*Zoe*	(?) . . Behind the plaster, something like that.
84	*Tom*	Yeah, but what's a jig?
85	*Graham*	That's a dance isn't it? Irish sort of song.
86	*Tom*	Is it? No it isn't, it's a jog.
87	*Zoe*	'Lost score of a jig' means they can't find the music.
88	*Graham*	A jig, 'the lost score of a jig. '. . . A jig, 'the lost score of a jig.' The score is the piece of music and the jig's a dance.
89	*Zoe*	So you can't do it if you can't find it.
90	*Tom*	The last bit of a dance, yeah?
91	*Graham*	So the lost score – the score is what it's written on – it's the music.
92	*Zoe*	So they lost it, nobody knows what it is.
93	*Tom*	Eh?
94	*Nick*	Everything's coming to an end at the end of the day.
95	*Tom*	Oh yes, sort of—
96	*Nick*	Everything's sort of slowing down till it stops.
97	*Tom*	Yeah.
98	*Graham*	The day, the day's a sort of a dance –
99	*Tom*	And dusk's the last bit of it.

Tom's puzzlement is caused essentially by a vocabulary difficulty: he simply does not know the meaning of the word 'jig' though the others, who do, are quick to help him. Zoe's uncertainty about the word 'carp' has already been noted and it may be that Tom's difficulty here might also not have been so apparent in a whole class lesson. The need to know is strong throughout these exchanges and is characteristic of this and many other tapes, seemingly overcoming any inhibitions that might have been felt. One of the group, though, Lucy, rarely ventures herself very far. The pupils take over the teacher's role interrogating the text for themselves although, by virtue of being the initiators of the questions, they ask only those for which they perceive they need an answer. This is both a strength and a weakness. A sensitive teacher may be in a position to see those key questions that are not asked and to guide the group towards deeper understanding by prompting them. Nonetheless there is much evidence to support Douglas Barnes's view that 'most children can be far more self-responsible learners than most teachers allow'. It is perhaps even open to question whether much would have been gained by a teacher's correction of Tom's confusion of 'lost' and 'last' which is apparent at line 90 and persists throughout until line 99 with such a successful outcome. L. A. G. Strong's observation that 'a child's misconception may be of much greater value to him than the explanation which destroys it'[10] may be relevant here.

Clear explanation of one image proved difficult for the group:

100 *Graham* 'The deer on the . . .' What about 'The deer are on the the bare-blown hill/Like smiles on a nurse'?
101 *Zoe* I don't get that.
102 *Graham* No, it doesn't seem like all this. The others kind of relate – the cod, and the key in the purse, kind of relate more than 'The deer on . . .'

Graham is here seemingly pondering the internal consistency of the images but Tom is prompted by Graham's use of the word 'relate' to pick up the idea, first suggested in line 76 by Nick, that there is a overall pattern to the imagery:

103 *Tom* Yeah. What is . . . I mean it's got fish in all three here – 'The carp's in its depth/Like a planet in its heaven'; then

'The trout's in its hole/Like a chuckle in a sleeper' – erm – and 'The cod's in the tide rip/Like a key in a purse.' It must all relate somehow.

and so switches attention to the larger question:

104 *Graham* The first verse is always fish –
105 *Tom* You know . . . sort of tide.
106 *Zoe* Yes, the first bit of it.
107 *Graham* Yes, the first line. Up here you've got the first four lines then you've got fish.
108 *Zoe* The last one's always . . . a bird.
109 *Tom* Yeah, and then you've got –
110 *Zoe* Badger. – They're all the mammals.
111 *Tom* Yeah, and you've got a lot about steel in there as well. – The 'slow trap of steel' . . . erm . . . You got badger . . . 'jaws of a steel vice . . .'
112 *Graham* Badger –
113 *Zoe* Hare –
114 *Lucy* and deer.
115 *Tom* We're paying a lot of attention to what he's said.
116 *Nick* And music as well. (?). . . things, 'cos you've got a clock in its tower –
117 *Graham* It's all natural –
118 *Nick* – and sparrows in the ivy clump –
119 *Tom* Yeah, what about –
120 *Nick* Then it's got 'doll in its lace.'
121 *Zoe* It's sort of all relating where they live.
122 *Tom* Yeah, and music as well – 'like a viol in its case' –
123 *Graham* It all matches as if –
124 *Tom* – and, erm – 'lost score of a jig' –

125 *Graham*   It's nature going back to its
                home in the evening, the
                dusk.
126   *Zoe*   Yes.

There is a complex co-operative effort here with each child building upon the formulations and half spoken hints thrown out by others, so adding a further twist to what the Bullock report described as a spiral process:

> The effort to formulate a hypothesis, to put into words some possibility we have envisaged, results in a 'spelling out' to which we may then return, in the light of further experience and in search of further possibilities. By a kind of spiral the formulation itself becomes a source from which we draw further questions, fresh hypotheses. The statement we have made becomes an object to our contemplation and a spur to further thinking.[11]

With remarkable rapidity the group teases out much of the underlying structure of the poem's imagery, 'leapfrogging' excitedly through the piece and relating the insights of the moment to those insights that may have first been given tentative formulation a hundred lines earlier. Tom's observation that 'We're paying a lot of attention to what he's said', is made with innocent amazement at this apparently unusual circumstance: the children are quickened and sustained throughout by their own sense of discovery. Bruner remarked that 'a body of knowledge is given life and direction by the conjectures and dilemmas that brought it into being and sustained its growth'.[12] As the children unravel the complexities of the poem both in terms of its meaning and its structure, its feelings and its intention they perhaps become aware of the artist's 'conjectures and dilemmas' and glimpse some of the possibilities of poetry. On two fronts they are moving towards finding

that, as Lawrence suggested,

> The essential quality of poetry is that it makes a new effort of attention and 'discovers' a new world within the known world.[13]

It both 'discovers' and is discovered. For this and other groups the riddling quality of the imagery is an important spur to their engagement with the poem and is perhaps allied to the quality of 'mystery' which, Roy Fuller suggests, children 'sought and were fascinated by' in literature, particularly in the words and images of poetry, adding:

> I don't mean the poet should deliberately assume the magician's robes; rather the craft itself, the effort of trying to master it, leads him to shapes and colours and meanings he never imagined were in him.[14]

As for the poet, so for the reader. Sharing each other's insights into the text develops individual confidence to make meanings in a way they had never imagined was in them before.

Reading is a participatory act as well as an individual one: in reading we are creators too. As Dewey remarks

> For to perceive, a beholder must create his own experience. And his creation must include relations comparable to those which the original producer underwent. They are not the same in any literal sense. But with the perceiver, as with the artist, there must be an ordering of the elements of the whole that is in form, although not in details, the same as the process of organization the creator of the work consciously experienced. Without an act of recreation the object is not perceived as a work of art.[15]

Dewey was, of course, concerned with the process that takes place within the individual beholder of any work of art but something analogous appears to be happening within the group response to the poem. Perhaps the need to 'voice' the poem by 'savouring' lines, murmuring them to themselves—much more than they would with a piece of prose — is indicative of this creation of experience. The impact of poetry is both cerebral through the sense of the words and emotional through sound, tone, colour and associations. Fragments of an almost involuntary interpretative performance result as, both individually and collectively, they seek to order their experience of the poem at different levels. The reader thus becomes very much a creative artist and the shared small group reading opens up many possible meanings, significances and interpretations that might remain inaccessible to the individual. This explicit group construction of meaning by these emergent readers is perhaps akin to the internal dialogue between reader and text that one might expect of the more sophisticated reader.

The meaning-making undertaken here and invited by the densely packed images and highly structured nature of this particular poem may sometimes appear to lie close to textual analysis or 'comprehension' of a conventional teacher directed kind and analysis, as Edwin Muir warned, is not without its dangers:

> Analysis, especially if it is applied
> too early, makes the poem into a
> problem instead of an experience.
> And if the beginner is unlucky it
> may become a problem before it has
> ever been an experience.[16]

Where this imposes a closed questioning mode of analysis with a teacher acting, in Rosen's phrase, as 'a sort of benevolent sheepdog'[17] then the limitations and dangers are clear: here, perhaps the distinction is less apparent, for these children appear to be framing their own

method of analysis as a mode of experiencing the poem. They are, it seems, moving away from both the fear of difficulty and from the teacher dependency noted by the *Secondary Survey* as major barriers to children's voluntary engagement with poetry.

> Many comments implied that pupils
> perceived poetry as something
> highly complex in expression and
> meaning and so they either felt in-
> adequate, without a teacher to
> mediate and explain, or were reluct-
> ant to embark independently on re-
> ading which required so much
> effort.[18]

The preconceived evaluation which is often unwittingly implicit in teachers' questioning runs counter to the pupils' evident need to move through the poem tentatively whilst developing and bringing to bear something of what Bruner calls a 'disciplined intuition'.[19] Poems are not merely 'puzzles in need of solutions', as Fox and Merrick point out[20], but many poems, particularly this one, invite an active and acknowledged engagement with that slippery 'goblin in a word which is its life and poetry'[21] and delight may sometimes lie in the encounter. Iser suggests that 'the reader's enjoyment begins when he himself becomes productive, i.e. when the text allows him to bring his own faculties into play', and author and reader share 'the game of the imagination'.[22] Iser had the individual reader in mind but sometimes the group is instrumental in bringing about a productive engagement that might well have eluded the individual reader. Consider the following exchange where Zoe tries over one of the lines reflectively and finds it promptly dismissed by Nick:

| 184 | *Zoe* | 'The past and the future/Are the jaws of a steel vice.' |
| 185 | *Nick* | That's pretty stupid. |

186	Tom	Yeah . . . Suppose it could mean the two things coming together.
187	Zoe	It's being held together.
188	Tom	Yeah. Well, the two things, the past and the future, coming together into the present –
189	Nick	Means you can't separate them. – You can't really, can you?
190	Zoe	Well, they're frozen together.
191	Nick	You can't distinguish between past and future. – As soon as you say 'past and future' it's the past, isn't it?
192	Zoe	You can think of it as all being –
193	Tom	You wouldn't know which was which, would you?
194	Graham	Because the future becomes the past and the past was the future.
195	Tom	Yeah. And the future and past mixed together becomes present.
196	Zoe	It's all sort of held together.

Nick at first rejects the image out of hand (line 185) and Tom tentatively offers an explanation (line 186) which is confidently confirmed by Zoe (line 187). Tom, in amplifying his original perception, causes Nick to engage with the line almost against his will (line 189) and a discussion which echoes Eliot's *Burnt Norton* ensues. Zoe and Nick between them bring the discussion back to the particular force of the image:

205	Nick	. . . they're probably hinting at next morning when everything starts again.
206	Zoe	Yeah, it's 'jaws of a steel vice' – you can't tell that you're not quite either can you? It's not –
207	?	It's closing down.
208	Nick	Because of the vice you can tell it's not going to be an everlasting –
209	Zoe	It's not the past, it's not the future, it's just now.
210	Graham	It's something in between.
211	Nick	It's sort of a vice. You can open it or something.
212	Tom	Yeah, and let it out.
213	Nick	All these things, where the things are staying, they're all things they can get out of.
214	Zoe	Yes, but they're not going to for a while, while it's cold.
215	Tom	Of course they do because they all go to sleep and they wake up and they all start afresh sort of thing.

The shared teasing out of meaning becomes in some measure itself an articulation of their experience of the line. Geraldine Murray suggested that 'until the mind can hold various ideas simultaneously, severally, and as a unity, it will not be able fully to respond to metaphor'.[23] It seems likely that, collectively, these children are moving towards such a capability and, ultimately, towards a fuller response. For Nick especially, bright though he is, the gentle re-direction of his sometimes mistaken perceptions by his peers is valuable. Here, Graham prompts him by mentioning the title of the poem:

288	Graham	'And the badger in its bedding' . . . That isn't really much to do with the freezing dusk.
289	Nick	Well, it's like the 'doll in its lace': it's got nothing to do with it.
290	Graham	It's called *The Warm and the Cold* but it's more about the dark . . .
291	Tom	The warm?

292	Graham	. . . the darkness and the . . .
293	Nick	The first four lines are talking about the cold and the next are about the warm.
294	Lucy	The warm.
295	Zoe	Yeah — all just nice and snug.
296	Lucy	Yeah!
297	Tom	Oh, yeah!
298	Nick	The first four lines are describing what's happening outside —
299	Zoe	— and then what's happening inside —
300	Lucy	— in their holes, in their homes —
301	Nick	— where it's freezing . . . Then the next describes it nice and warm inside.
302	Tom	Yeah! Yeah! Like 'a carp in its depth' — Right? — He's warm down there — Right? 'A planet in its heaven' — that's snug — yeah?

Nick immediately sees the structure of the verse as a result of Graham's musing and once more reverses his earlier dismissive attitude being willing to return to the text. The 'analytic competence' shown here goes beyond that associated with a standard comprehension exercise: there is no doubt from the tone of the exchanges that the children are inside the poem and full of delight. Even Lucy, a quiet and absorbed girl, cannot resist joining in excitedly and Tom rehearses the details (line 302) with evident pleasure.

Directly as a result of Nick's suggestion, Graham is able to make a significant observation about the closing lines which had caused them difficulty about one hundred exchanges earlier in their discussion:

| 304 | Graham | He's done it again there if you think about it — 'Such a frost/The flimsy moon/Has lost her wits' — |

305	Zoe	— and then 'the sweating farmers' —
306	Graham	Yeah, and then he breaks it with 'a star falls.'
307	Zoe	Yes.
308	Graham	'A star falls . . .'
309	Tom	I wonder why he did that — break it with 'A star falls'?
310	Zoe	Why is there 'A star falls'?
311	Nick	He's just describing it as at night time there's two totally different scenes on the world —
312	Zoe	Inside and outside, sort of thing. But why this 'A star falls'?
313	Tom	I think that's probably —
314	Nick	— to break it.
315	Zoe	Maybe . . . yes.
316	Tom	Yeah, I think —
317	Zoe	So it doesn't go straight into it.
318	Tom	Yeah, I think that's something that happens. It's away —
319	Nick	It's changing it —
320	Tom	— from the general poem, so he's put it somewhere else —
321	Zoe	Yes.
322	Tom	— as if it doesn't fit properly.
323	Graham	He doesn't need that but it adds something to the poem.
324	Tom	Yeah.
325	Zoe	Well it, it —
326	Tom	Perhaps —
327	Graham	If you saw it without it, without that bit in there —
328	Zoe	— you might read it all as one thing. He wants it to be two nasty verses, two separate little bits.
329	Tom	Yeah, I wonder why? I mean he —
330	Nick	The last two verses explain the whole, the whole thing.
331	Tom	Yeah, he could've —
332	Zoe	They sum it up completely —

333	*Nick*	**By** them being so totally separate —
334	*Zoe*	They do sum it up.
335	*Nick*	— they fit into the pattern of the whole poem.

With the insights gained from the others and the gentle pressure to make sense of the text, Nick is once more brought to focus more thoughtfully on what is before him and moves a considerable way from his earlier puzzlement at line 257: 'I can't see why he's stretched it out into three verses and then crammed something totally different into two.' The group's new and stronger awareness of pattern and structure gained in the exchange at lines 288–303 has illuminated their understanding of the final seven lines of the poem and demonstrates a growing confidence in expressing their feeling for changes of pace, tone and mood. 'A literary text implies a transformation towards meaningfulness,' suggests Holland,[24] and notes that though a text has direction — beginning, progressing and ending — 'the skilled reader also gives the text meaning by making connections between all parts of the text, regardless of direction or position.' Together the group are learning to become skilled readers by making such connections and relating repeated images and structural patterns as they perceive the poem's underlying unity. The group sense the appropriateness of the lines and respond to the satisfaction they offer as an ending.

Less than one third of the discussion is reproduced here and nearly all of it shows characteristics similar to those observed above. The evidence of this and many other tapes suggests that the non-threatening workshop atmosphere of a tape recorded group given a lightly structured task is a particularly suitable way of balancing the need to explore the text with the need to preserve its appeal. It is, of course, only one possible approach and it is not without its problems: points that a teacher might have picked up are missed, lines are misinterpreted; even in a small group not everyone, as has been seen, takes a full part. Taping groupwork can be time-consuming and difficult to organise and, unless the teacher embarks on an unrealistic programme of taping and listening to every group, everything that goes on cannot be monitored. Experience suggests that such close monitoring may be neither necessary nor desirable and that in practice it may be possible for each member of an average class to undertake taped groupwork of this kind about twice per term. Several teachers have noted an increased willingness on the part of pupils to take part in discussion of all kinds following taped small groupwork: the teacher of the pupils whose conversation has been followed above remarked on the much higher degree of involvement and confidence shown by individual members of the group during class discussion after this, their first, small group session.

There can, of course, be problems of control with unsupervised talk but experience with a wide range of groups of all ages and abilities indicates that these are not as common as some teachers fear. It may be that the presence of the tape recorder has a positive effect in focussing the pupils' attention at an early stage and in encouraging more purposeful talk: certainly most of the children believe this to be true. There is no doubt that in these circumstances they feel themselves engaged on a 'real' task and this is bound up closely with the view that their perceptions are valued rather than evaluated. There is, in general, both a greater opportunity and a greater willingness to take risks, declare ignorance, co-operate with and listen to others and, above all, to build on others' insights. The poem is given close and sustained attention and it appears that the pupils' comments gain steadily in length, complexity and depth of understanding as the discussion progresses.

The pupils' talk, both within the taped session and afterwards, made it clear that they themselves valued certain things very highly:

1 The opportunity to share the poem and to

make sense of the piece together, thus making the task less daunting

2 The opportunity to take responsibility for their own learning and the sense of being trusted and of respect for their response that this implies

3 The opportunity to develop their own lines of thought without a teacher dominating discussion, legitimising, licensing and seeking always to unify response by means of 'agreed' interpretations

4 The opportunity to become productive through a creative engagement with the text

5 The opportunity to perceive themselves becoming productive in this way and to reflect on the processes by which they acquire their experience of the poem

6 The opportunity — rare in most lessons — to spend as much time as was necessary in coming to terms with the poem, to find sufficient 'mental space'

7 The opportunity to talk without the insistence that writing is the only legitimate response

The combination of mental space and gentle pressure inherent in the situation moves the pupils towards developing their own strategies for engaging with poetry whilst keeping their responses personal and unfragmented. As Tom puts it:

504   *Tom*   . . . I wouldn't know what the bloody 'ell it was on about unless we'd 'ad a pow-wow like this . . . I'm sorry but I just wouldn't, would I? Unless we went into a deep discussion which 'as taken us about a quarter of an hour, I mean, I wouldn't . . .

505   *Nick*   Quarter of an hour? It's taken longer than that.

506   *Tom*   'as it? Oh, about 'alf an hour then.

507 *Graham*   You can't tell because you've been talking about it: you've been *thinking* about something.

CHAPTER FOUR

Other Voices

'The more you speak about it, the better it seems to be.'

(First year boy)

The third year group's encounter with the poem described in the previous chapter, partly because of the nature of the poem, partly, one suspects because of the nature of the participants in the discussion, stresses particularly the poem's structure and patterning. It may be that the finely balanced mechanism of the verse is important in winning the initial respect and ultimate admiration of the group. It is by no means all that the poem has to offer but it is a 'way in' which they develop for themselves and which engages their concentrated attention. It is perhaps relevant in this context that Ray Tarleton, reporting his research for the Schools Council Project on Children's Thinking, remarks

> The most interesting finding and indeed the one that recurred again and again, was the fact that these eleven year olds not only have a strong sense of form but they regard it as the most important feature of poetry. From their discussion and their writing it comes

across as an essential quality, communicating meaning and enjoyment. It is the instrument of meaning rather than a by-product of the writing. For them the focus is on the way something is written. Form is a means of understanding reality and understanding the world. [1]

Although Tarleton is reporting on younger children, something of the same approach appears to be observable in the third year groups. All groups working with this poem show a degree of concern for structural features and it would seem absurd to regard such practical concern as being in opposition to an expression of 'feeling': the two elements are more usefully seen as complementary rather than antipathetic, inseparably fused together. The Gulbenkian Foundation report, *The Arts in Schools,* notes that 'Arts are not outpourings of emotion. They are disciplined forms of inquiry and expression through which to organise feelings and ideas about experience'. [2] From their conversation it is clear that these pupils are developing the beginnings of such an insight for themselves. Awareness of it finds expression in many different and often quite unexpected ways.

One group – all girls this time – from a third year class in another school began by declaring a general dislike of all poetry yet found that the piece won them over almost against their will. They finally made the poem their own by spontaneously arranging a re-reading of it which accommodated and gave expression to their earlier insights about both its technical structure and its mood:

173	*Nicky*	I think it's quite good.
174	*Sally*	I like it 'cos it rhymes.
175	*Pat*	It's got some quite good comparisons in it really.
176	*Carol*	I think it's a bit old-fashioned.
177	*Pat*	I think it's clever.
178	*Carol*	It's clever, yeah, but even so it doesn't really appeal to me.
179	*Pat*	You don't get poems up to date, do you?
180	*Nicky*	Yes you do.
181	*Sally*	At first I didn't really like it but once you've worked it out it's really clever.
182	*P.&N.*	Yeah, Yeah.
183	*Sally*	Yeah, it means . . . it rhymes and it's got a definite rhythm but then it's still a good poem.
184	*Pat*	It's a good poem with the fishes and then the animals . . Yeah, it's clever having done that . . . he or she or whoever. The comparisons must have taken a hell of a lot of working out, don't you reckon? I do.

There is a certain admiration for the poet's craft, grudgingly given in one case, but it is a starting point and the 'working out', however far short it may fall of an interpretation of the poem at its deepest levels, allows a positive set to develop towards it and a sense of personal investment which carries them on to the next stage:

185	*Nicky*	Shall we read it again?
186	*Pat*	Read it as a group . . . We could work something out.
187	*Sally*	Yeah, yeah. We could have somebody as a fish, somebody as an animal . . .
188	*Nicky*	Yeah, that would be good.
189	*Sally*	Somebody could do the bits in between . . .
190	*Nicky*	In between, yeah.
191	*Pat*	Somebody could do the first bit, then the next bit, then someone could do the last bit.
192	*Sally*	No you have to have the first four lines all the same really, aren't they?
193	*?*	Yeah.
194	*Sally*	'Freezing dusk is closing . . .' in the same tone of voice you'd have to do it.
195	*Pat*	Then you could have the carp, then the animal, then the insect and you could have the bird.
196	*Carol*	Why don't you just read it? It's easier.
197	*Pat*	So you do the first four lines, she does the fish, I'll do the animal. She does the insect, you do the bird, then she does the next four lines.
198	*?*	Yeah, OK.
199	*Carol*	Where's the insect?
200	*Nicky*	Oh, the butterfly and the snail and the viol in its case and the fly.
201	*Pat*	And the thing you do in the first verse, you must do in the second in the same tone. Do you understand?
202	*Nicky*	Well if you . . . If it ends up that Carol is doing the owl or something but the last time Pat was doing the weather, it goes back to Pat again. You want the same person doing the weather . . .

203	*Sally*	Oh, I see, OK.
204	*Nicky*	You're doing the weather all the time then.
205	*Sally*	OK. All ready then?
206	*Pat*	No, stop a minute . . . You could say 'The Warm' and we could say 'The Cold'.
207	*Nicky*	When you say 'Warm' say it in a nice tone of voice and 'Cold' cold. OK? Ready? (*Poem read aloud as arranged*) I reckon we should . . .
208	*Sally*	Yeah, if we'd had five people like we were meant to then it would've worked perfectly.
209	*Pat*	And the last bit one person should've said 'A star falls'.
210	*Sally*	Yeah.
211	*Nicky*	Yeah, I like that poem actually.
212	*Carol*	Yeah, it is good.
211	*Pat*	It's good the way they do the end bit – they sort of do the cold bit and then 'a star falls' and then the hot bit.

There are still misunderstandings and uncertainties but all, even Carol, seem to be much nearer to 'possessing' the poem, making it their own, than they were at the outset. In the course of their earlier discussion they have invested a great deal of themselves in the poem and consequently feel a claim on it and in particular on the parts each has helped to elucidate. There is considerable excitement and enthusiasm as they organise the reading with all the pupils coming alive and responding to the poem at a deeper level than they had been able to express previously. The style of the reading and the care for tone as at lines 204/5 and 209 show a response to qualities other than those previously recognised only by the word 'clever'. The articulation of their response leads them in further than they had intended – the group showed a marked antipathy at the outset and was at best lukewarm. This second reading, arranged by them, is an important stage in the evolution of their enjoyment and understanding. They have put the poem back together and felt it work with a new force which they have themselves released. Intellectually the poem leaves them in some confusion but a drive towards ordering the experience through their recreative reading is apparent. After the reading, Nicky asks if there are any comparisons the others really like and provokes a warm response:

214	*Sally*	I like a 'badger in its bedding' and 'loaf in the oven'.
215	*?*	(*various murmurs of agreement*) Yeah, that's a really good comparison. yeah. yeah.
216	*Pat*	I like 'But the carp is in its depth/Like a planet in its heaven.
217	*Sally*	Yeah, and also I like 'money in a pig'.
218	*Nicky*	Yeah, I knew you liked that . . . I was going to say that.
219	*Sally*	I don't know, they're all really good like 'key in a purse' 'cause it sort of changes, 'cause one minute it's about nature and things outside and then . . .
220	*Carol*	Some of the comparisons are really weird.
221	*Nicky*	I like 'The flies are behind the plaster/Like the lost score of a jig' 'cause when you've worked it out it's a good one.
222	*Sally*	Yeah, it is a good one but I don't know if we got the right meaning.
223	*Nicky*	I think it is right though.
224	*Sally*	Yeah, it is quite good . . . sort of buzzing around out of time
225	*Nicky*	This here: 'sparrows are in the ivy clump . . .' Oh, you said that one, didn't you?

226	*?Pat*	They're all good I think.
227	*?*	Mmm.
228	*Sally*	I don't know about the last bit – having it differently, you know, three then one then three, 'cause the first three verses are exactly the same, rhyming exactly the same place etc. . . .
229	*?*	Yeah.
230	*Pat*	I think it's really good.
231	*Nicky*	It's turned out really well.
232	*Sally*	So do I.
233	*Carol*	So do I.

These comments are all very specific, the best indication we have as to their deeper understanding of the poem comes from their reading. Perhaps the most important thing to come out of this joint creative re-reading and its attendant discussion, is not some orthodox 'understanding' of a cognitive kind but a realisation that interpretation is permissible, that it is not fixed, and that it can be an enjoyable activity. Perhaps Pat and friends in the exchanges above or Tom, Zoe and the rest in the lengthy discussion quoted earlier, although both stimulated initially by the discovery of a sense of a hidden order within the poem and a desire to tease out meaning, are beginning to find, in Coleridge's words, that 'The reader should be carried forward, not merely or chiefly by the mechanical impulse of curiosity, or by a restless desire to arrive at the final solution; but the pleasurable activity of mind excited by the attractions of the journey itself.'[3]

Sensing that the poem is deeper than they can express is not necessarily an admission of incomprehension but may be the beginnings of a deeper understanding.

Peter Abbs, discussing the writing process, notes that 'creative attending often begins with what is imperfect: with notes, jottings, hints at meaning rather than meaning itself. It is through these fragments that the representative art finally emerges. Through the struggle of building and discarding, creating and destroying . . . the writer hopes to attain the animated symmetry of art.'[4] Group engagement with a poem would appear to encourage a similar imperfect, tentative exploration, moving always towards coherence, pattern and form. Abbs continues by suggesting that 'The cry "only the best" is important but it can give birth prematurely to a hyper-critical attitude and engender in the would-be-creator an impending sense of sterility.' This comment too seems relevant to much of the talk about poetry as well as to the writing of it. As Rosenblatt comments, the social and intellectual atmosphere can be such that 'good literature' becomes 'almost by definition, works accessible only to the elitist critic or literary historian, and this leads the average reader to assume that he simply is not capable of participating in them.'[5] She had in mind somewhat older students in the context in which she was writing, but I think it important that we recognise that the process starts typically at a very early stage in the secondary school.

Making a poem one's own rather than making it as the school or the examination system is perceived to require, is difficult. The nature of most secondary school learning is still opposed to such open-endedness and tends towards the neat, right answer for which, by definition, 'only the best' will serve. Classroom pressures, and in particular, the requirement in examination years to tick off points, to produce, may lead in time to knowledgeable talk such as the following, fairly typical, opening exchanges from a Lower Sixth A-level English group tackling the same poem:

| 1 | *Bill* | It's a simple play on his title 'The Warm and the Cold' You can see the difference between the first part of each verse and the second part, yes? The first he seems to describe the coldness of the air, the evening or whatever, and then he says but the carp's |

warm, the planet's warm in its heaven, the loaf's warm in its oven, i.e. the warm and the cold, yes? And he does this with each verse, saying it's getting very cold, it's getting colder as the evening progresses, but such and such is warm whatever it is. And he does this by absolutely saturating the poem with similes and metaphors with which to describe how something is warm or something is cold. All the second part of it is also a long simile.

2 *Sheila* That bit, the first part of it . . .

3 *Bridie* That's what we ought to have a look at.

4 *Gary* 'Freezing dusk is closing/Like a slow trap of steel' — that's a simile. 'On trees and roads and hills and all That can no longer feel' — that's personification. Metaphor is when it's like a simile but it doesn't say 'as' or 'like' in it. And these say 'like'. So it's simile, simile, simile simile, break, break, simile —

5 *Bill* You're right actually.

6 *Gary* It's simile, break, simile, break . . . all the way down except for the personification at the top.

It is undeniably businesslike; the group rapidly grasp one aspect of the poem's structure and are able to make far more sophisticated assumptions about the techniques of poetry than can the younger pupils. Their training has, in a sense, paid off, but is there something chilling about this cut and dried approach? Is this the end of teaching poetry? Is much of our teaching tending, in Leavis's words to 'abet the reader's desire to arrive without having travelled'[6], short–circuiting the process of responding actively and personally to a poem? Sheila and

another girl are uneasy about Bill's entirely mechanistic approach; they like the poem and, though they cannot claim in their words 'to understand it properly . . . There's something about it.' Sheila isn't entirely sure of her reasons for thinking so however and at one point remarks 'Because we've been given it you expect it to have some deep meaning.' Bill promptly takes her up:

1 *Bill* Why does there have to be a meaning behind it though? Why can't it just be a simple backing up of the title 'The Warm and the Cold'?

2 *Sheila* Because you don't study that kind of thing, you just read them. . . .

3 *Ben* Why not? Why can't we just accept for once that we've got a simple poem? . . .

4 *Sheila* Because it's not a simple world, and it's Monday and we wouldn't have a simple poem on a Monday.

Both Sheila's comments are devoid of cynicism, registering a realistic awareness of the realities of life in an examination class. The freshness of approach readily found in younger pupils is not easily retained in the face of such pressure and often pupils in the examination years speak with less spontaneity, more awareness of the 'acceptable' register of critical comment and of teacherly expectations. In Witkin's terms, 'objective experience' may be valued above subjective experience and whilst many teachers endorse the notion of self-expression in both talk and writing they are understandably wary of it where examination classes are concerned. As a result,

Too often what passes for creative response to works of literature is merely stylised analysis, predictable and elaborated 'critic talk' embodying those canned nuances that announce only the worldliness of the writer or speaker involved.[7]

It is a situation with which those working with teachers on initial training courses are all too familiar. Two years in the sixth form and a further three years in higher education instead of liberating, can often have the effect of constricting response. Few postgraduate groups discussing poems are as interesting, as open as the perfectly ordinary third years we have heard. If we do not have a care they, in their turn, will perpetuate the problem with their own sixth forms as they attempt to teach poetry. Louise Rosenblatt observes the same phenomenon when she writes that those most extensively 'trained' in literature

> are often the most reluctant to yield to the need to share experiences. They have become insecure, fearful that a spontaneous response will 'give them away', reveal their failure to make the 'correct' or at least sufficiently sophisticated interpretation.[8]

Younger pupils are often very much less self-conscious, willing to explore and to relate their reading, often anecdotally, to their own experience. They will more readily draw on their personal and intuitive knowledge than will their older counterparts trained to value objectivity and detachment.

The risk taken in sharing such knowledge seems to be greater as pupils progress through the school, and is greater too in the face of a large group. Peer group approval becomes increasingly important as pupils move into adolescence and, to a large extent, it replaces approval from the teacher. It is difficult to find common ground between any group of thirty; more so if they are unwilling to break the tacit agreement that involvement, particularly with poetry, is a sign of weakness.

* * *

In this context it is perhaps helpful to look at three transcripts from a group of first year pupils. The first transcript is a response to John Walsh's poem *The Bully Asleep*. This poem was deliberately chosen because of Douglas Barnes' well-known account of using the same piece with a similar group some years ago[9]: it was felt that it might be interesting to put some other responses alongside those recorded by him. There were five pupils in the group, three girls and two boys. As before, the poem was first read by the teacher, the four very general instructions were given and the group left alone, this time in a corner of the classroom, to talk.

1	*Philip*	I didn't like that poem that much.
2	*Rachel*	I did. It was a good revenge.
3	*Mary*	A what?
4	*Rachel*	Revenge.
5	*Philip*	I didn't. I thought it was a bit horrible, you see.
6	*Rachel*	R-e-v-e-n-g-e. Revenge.
7	*Mary*	All right, we know how to spell it.
8	*Liz*	What?
9	*Rachel*	R-e-v-e-n-g-e. Revenge.
10	*Liz*	You mean you liked the revenge? . . . Flippin' 'arry, you're going barmy.
11	*Rachel*	I think this is really good. They plotted it out . . (*laughter*)
12	*Mary*	The teacher, Miss Andrews, wouldn't let him sleep on, would she?
13	*Rachel*	I don't know.
14	*Liz*	Pardon?
15	*Rachel*	Mary said the teacher wouldn't let him sleep on, would she?
16	*Robert*	No.
17	*Liz*	She wouldn't.
18	*Philip*	That's a bit silly. I did that when I was a little infant and I was . . .

The Bully Asleep

One afternoon, when grassy
Scents through the classroom crept,
Bill Craddock laid his head
Down on his desk, and slept.

The children came round him;
Jimmy, Roger, and Jane;
They lifted his head timidly
And let it sink again.

'Look, he's gone sound asleep, Miss,'
Said Jimmy Adair;
'He stays up all the night, you see;
His mother doesn't care.'

'Stand away from him, children.'
Miss Andrews stooped to see.
'Yes, he's asleep; go on
With your writing, and let him be.'

'Now's a good chance!' whispered Jimmy;
And he snatched Bill's pen and hid it.
'Kick him under the desk, hard;
He won't know who did it.

Fill all his pockets with rubbish—
Paper, apple-cores, chalk.'
So they plotted, while Jane
Sat wide-eyed at their talk.

Not caring, not hearing
Bill Craddock he slept on;
Lips parted, eyes closed —
Their cruelty gone.

'Stick him with pins!' muttered Roger.
'Ink down his neck!' said Jim.
But Jane, tearful and foolish,
Wanted to comfort him.

John Walsh

19	*Robert*	Mrs B. (*their teacher*) wouldn't; she'd wake you up. I'd wake you up.
20	*Philip*	You'd get a letter back, you'd get a letter back to say 'look, your children shouldn't be sleeping'—just like that.
21	*Liz*	I know. That was a bit funny, but . . .
22	*Philip*	I really like that.
23	*Rachel*	It's a good revenge.
24	*Robert*	Good plot, eh?
25	*Rachel*	I think it's really good.
26	*Robert*	If I was that bully, I'd take my hands off the desk. I'd kick all you lot.
27	*Philip*	'But Jane . . .' But here it says 'But Jane, tearful and foolish, wanted to comfort him.'
28	*Rachel*	Yeah, you can't comfort him if he's asleep.
29	*Philip*	I know, doesn't it sound daft?
30	*Rachel*	Yeah, like you.
31	*Mary*	She felt sorry for him.
32	*Liz*	I wouldn't.
33	*Robert*	'Now's a good chance, whispered Jimmy . . .'
34	*Philip*	If you kicked someone, you'd probably know who it was 'cos it would have to be one of those two or three you see.
35	*Liz*	Yes, but he wouldn't really know, would he?
36	*Mary*	He wouldn't know whether . . .
37	*Rachel*	It could have been the teacher.
38	*Philip*	If he was a bully, he would have beaten them up.
39	*Liz*	I know, but the teacher wouldn't let them . . . the children.
40	*Rachel*	How do you know she wouldn't?
41	*Liz*	It's the children they're talking about, not the teacher.
42	*Philip*	Oh dear. She stays up all night, you see, his mother . . .
43	*Robert*	He'd beat them all up.
44	*Liz*	Bet you his mum didn't care.
45	*Philip*	My mum cares.
46	*Liz*	So does my mum. She says

'back at half past nine' and spoils the party.

47	*Philip*	My dad isn't half strict.
48	*Mary*	Do you like it then Liz?
49	*Liz*	Yes, it's great.
50	*Rachel*	My dad isn't.
51	*Mary*	My mum makes me go to bed at night.
52	*Rachel*	My dad doesn't. He's not as strict as my mum.
53	*Robert*	Good revenge, really.
54	*Philip*	Depends which one of mine you mean, really.
55	*Mary*	I suppose it is quite good.
56	*Philip*	I've got two dads, you see.
57	*Liz*	Yeah, he's probably bullied on them and everything.
58	*Rachel*	Yeah, so they want their revenge.
59	*Robert*	They just want to do back what he's done to them.
60	*Philip*	The more you speak about it the better it seems to be.
61	*Liz*	Do unto others as you want done to you.
62	*(General agreement)*	Yeah, yeah.

The children, particularly Philip, move towards the centre of the poem from quite different starting points, bringing their personal experience to bear and, in some cases, modifying their initial response to the piece in the light of others perceptions.

The interaction is interesting. Rachel, bubbly, lively, something of a joker and always anxious to be noticed, sees only the superficial 'fun' of the situation and identifies wholly with the notion of revenge. Philip on the other hand, a boy who is rather a loner, switched off and typically a non-contributor in class, responds to the poem on a much deeper personal level. His opening comment at line 1 ('I didn't like that poem that much') is not negative as it may at first appear to be, for, as he makes clear at line 5, he takes the part of the tormented rather than that of the tormentors and his unhappiness

stems not so much from the poem as from his feeling of sympathy for the bully. Rachel goes her own way, unrepentant to the last, trying unsuccessfully to focus attention on her jokey comments. The others brush these aside, first placing the poem in the context of their own school experience, (e.g. lines 12, 15, 19, 20) by means of anecdote, then establishing what actually happened, with Philip at line 27 seizing on the key line 'But Jane, tearful and foolish,/Wanted to comfort him.' Finally, at lines 41 – 62 they generalise their interpretation of the poem in terms of their own home and family experience, a wider understanding of human nature and of the nature of forgiveness.

Philip's comment 'I know, doesn't it sound daft', is, judging from its tone, quite clearly a public defence against the sentiment which has touched him and his realisation at line 42 'Oh, dear. She stays up all night you see, his mother . . .' is uttered with a warmth that indicates the depth of his feeling. A careful reading of the remainder of his comments shows only too clearly why he should be so deeply involved with the story. For him the poem has opened up an area of sympathy and understanding the worth of which cannot be quantified. The others are drawn into his reading of the poem in some degree and the closing murmurs of agreement with Liz's final comment are heartfelt. Listening with half an ear to Rachel's flip comments, one might have been inclined to dismiss the conversation as trivial but, as so often, it works at several levels, some deeper than others. In the normal way of classroom organisation we do not have time to hear what is really being said.

Philip's dawning realisation, 'the more you speak about it, the better it seems to be,' spoken in a tone of mild surprise, with a sense of having made a personal discovery, is perhaps the most eloquent justification for this way of working. It would be overstating the case to say that in these exchanges there is evidence of the poem having a 'radical effect' on the children's perceptions but it is possible to sense something of what Whitehead suggests when he writes:

> What matters in our poetry lessons is the occasion when, for someone at least, reading a poem is felt to be important in a personal sense, a significant mode of experience, impinging on the life within and radically affecting it. This is clearly different from taking a poem as material for study, whether linguistic, historical, aesthetic, biographical, psychological or what have you. [10]

There is a close attention paid to the words on the page but just as important is the concern for what the poem brings to the surface in each individual reader. It may be a truism to state that as we read poems so they read us but unless this is the case there seems to be precious little justification for the activity in the first place. There is no overriding concern in these first year pupils for a 'correct' reading, no fear of getting it wrong and indeed no notion as yet that these things might come to matter. Louise Rosenblatt again seems to have got it entirely right when she states:

> What each reader makes of the text is, indeed, *for him* the poem, in the sense that this is his only direct perception of it. No one else can read it for him. He may learn indirectly about others' experiences with the text; he may come to see that his own was confused or impoverished, and he may be stimulated to call forth from the text a better poem. But this he must do himself, and only what he himself experiences in relation to the text is — again let us underline — for *him* the work. [11]

With emergent readers, learning how to engage with a text, it seems that the willing support and non-threatening atmosphere of the group can be invaluable in opening up possibilities of aesthetic response without, as is so often the case in the teacher directed discussion, pre-empting or dictating it.

The second transcript is of the same first year group discussing Harold Munro's sensuous poem *Milk For The Cat*. [12] Conditions for the recording were exactly as before though, as becomes clear from the discussion, the initial reading of the poem was perhaps a shade self-indulgent:

1	*Liz*	It was good that.
2	*Mary*	It was good.
3	*Rachel*	Yes, it explains the cat very well . . . just hit the nail on the head, it did.
4	*Philip*	Because the point is as if, as if the cat, as if he's a little er . . .
5	*Robert*	. . . kitten, and the table's a great big load of . . . I mean sort of . . . clouds.
6	*Liz*	Yeah.
7	*Philip*	Out of thin air, like a sort of giant or something. And she sort of thinks 'come on, where's my milk?' and then there's this great big flying saucer comes down with milk.
8	*Robert*	Whee!
9	*Philip*	And a sea comes down . . .
10	*Mary*	Pussy . . .
11	*Robert*	Or the full moon dropping out of the . . .
12	*Philip*	Yeah.
13	*Robert*	. . . sky. Coming down. It lands and she . . .
14	*Liz*	Doesn't remind me of that.
15	*Rachel*	I really think that one's good.
16	*Robert*	Yeah. It reminds me of all those people sitting at table . . .
17	*Philip*	It's sort of as if you were the cat yourself.

18	*Liz*	It's funny that because I was born on Friday 13th and we found a black cat when I was born on Friday 13th the black cat.
19	*Rachel*	You poor thing!
20	*Mary*	What month?
21	*Liz*	April.
22	*Philip*	I think that this was a very good poem because it sort of made you think . . . you were the cat. And you could tell just how it was before tea, creeping out and things.
23	*Robert*	Yeah.
24	*Philip*	Mmm. (*pretends to be cat*) 'these people, they never give me my tea.'
25	*Robert*	At first it sounds like he's stalking the people . . .
26	*Philip*	Yeah.
27	*Robert*	. . . and it isn't, it's stalking the milk.
28	*Philip*	What I think's good . . .
29	*Rachel*	I think it's a really good poem.
30	*Philip*	. . . the cat, when it comes in at first, seems as if it's got all the time for its milk . . .
31	*Mary*	Milk. Yeah.
32	*Philip*	. . . and then, later on, it thinks 'I must hurry' and then it comes back to what it was in the end.
33	*Mary*	Mmm.
34	*Liz*	It's sly and everything.
35	*Philip*	Do you agree with me?
36	*Rachel*	What's that where 'two old ladies stroke their silk'?
37	*Robert*	'She buries her chin in the creamy sea . . .'
38	*Rachel*	Could that be where they're wearing silk scarves or silk dresses they sit there going (*mimes stroking action*)
39	*Liz*	No . . .
40	*Philip*	It's more as if the whole family

Milk for the Cat

When the tea is brought at five o'clock,
  And all the neat curtains are drawn with care,
The little black cat with bright green eyes
  Is suddenly purring there.

At first she pretends, having nothing to do,
  She has come in merely to blink by the grate,
But, though tea may be late or the milk may be sour,
  She is never late.

And presently her agate eyes
  Take a soft large milky haze,
And her independent casual glance
  Becomes a stiff hard gaze.

Then she stamps her claws or lifts her ears
  Or twists her tail and begins to stir,
Till suddenly all her lithe body becomes
  One breathing trembling purr.

The children eat and wriggle and laugh;
  The two old ladies stroke their silk:
But the cat is grown small and thin with desire,
  Transformed to a creeping lust for milk.

The white saucer like some full moon descends
  At last from the clouds of the table above;
She sighs and dreams and thrills and glows,
  Transfigured with love.

She nestles over the shining rim,
  Buries her chin in the creamy sea;
Her tail hangs loose; each drowsy paw
  Is doubled under each bending knee.

A long dim ecstasy holds her life;
  Her world is an infinite shapeless white,
Till her tongue has curled the last holy drop,
  Then she sinks back into the night.

Draws and dips her body to heap
  Her sleepy nerves in the great arm-chair,
Lies defeated and buried deep
  Three or four hours unconscious there.

Harold Monro

		were old ladies.
41	*Liz*	. . . no it's like the coat, the coat's all . . .
42	*Robert*	No, it's like children have come to stay at their grandma's or something.
43	*Rachel*	Yeah.
44	*Liz*	I think this is really good.
45	*Robert*	Yeah.
46	*Philip*	I think it's a very good poem.
47	*Mary*	(*pretends to be cat*) 'Five O'clock . . . miaow . . . Do it . . . Do it! It's to be on the dot.'
48	*Robert*	It's like it's going to work to drink some milk, or something.
49	*Philip*	I think it's good 'cos it's . . . Mr Benton thinks it's good 'cos he thinks that . . . erm . . . taking it from Mr Benton's point of view that . . . 'e thinks it's good because it makes you think that you're a cat and that you're sort of its eyes . . . and then it suddenly goes on to what the cat does . . . creeps about (*pretends to be cat*) 'Where's my milk?'
50	*Rachel*	Creeps about, 'Where's my milk?'
51	*Robert*	Creeps about, 'Where's my milk?'
52	*Liz*	I suppose it makes you feel all lazy.
53	*Philip*	At first it makes you feel lazy, then it sort of brings you round sort of saying ''cos here's milk', making you more sort of . . .
54	*Robert*	Alert.
55	*Philip*	Yeah, alert and suspicious and then it makes you fall back into that drowsy. . .
56	*Robert*	It sounds like a stately home . . . all the

		neat curtains and things. (*Inaudible*) . . . It's like the Queen.
57	*Liz*	Yeah, proud.
58	*Robert*	The Queen coming to tea on 'er 'orse! (*Laughter*)
59	*Rachel*	It's as if it rules the world — all proud and it needs its milk.
60	*Philip*	But when it doesn't get its stuff, it's sort of (*sighs sadly*) 'Aah'.
61	*Mary*	'And thrills and glows . . .'
62	*Robert*	It doesn't get its milk so it claws the old ladies. (*Laughs, pretends to be cat*) 'Give me my milk goddesses!' . . . 'thrills and glows, transfigured by love . . .' Loves its cream.
63	*Rachel*	Like this . . . 'she sighs' . . . aah. . . 'and dreams' . . . mmm
64	*Philip*	And it licks up its milk (*makes lapping noises*).
65	*Robert*	I used to wonder what it would be like being a dog when you lick up your . . .
66	*Philip*	My sister does that.
67	*Liz*	They don't lick it like that though . . . they sort of flick it under their tongue.
68	*Philip*	I tried it once and it went all over my face.

Clearly the children are inside the poem and delighted by it from the outset. They recognise the cat's behaviour from their own observation and experience — 'it explains the cat very well' — and they enjoy reconstructing the situation in their own terms. Again, Philip plays an important part in realising the imagery of the poem; he is particularly sensitive to the scale of the scene and quickly adopts the viewpoint of the cat as it looks up towards the table (line 7) to see its 'flying saucer' descending. 'It's sort of as if you were the cat yourself,' he remarks, triggering that odd little anecdote from Liz about the finding of the black cat; an anecdote which is

not so out of place when taken in context with Philip's comment yet which, if overheard by a passing teacher, might be deemed irrelevant.

There is an immediate willingness to commit themselves to a judgement about the poem's worth and to explore it, savouring words and phrases, explicating and interpreting lines to each other and wanting to share the nature of their enjoyment with the group. They go straight to the heart of the poem—their first point of entry is at the sixth verse, not the first—because they can hold it as a complete experience. It is not perhaps claiming too much to say that they have experienced the poem almost physically, at first hand and any detailed explanation—of specific vocabulary, for example (what does 'agate' mean?)—would be unnecessary. They delight in re-telling the story, in turning it into a drama and re-enacting the scene, several times taking on the persona of the cat themselves.

* * *

The third transcript from this group is of their discussion of a poem which, in the normal run of things, would almost certainly not be attempted with first year pupils. The poem, Seamus Heaney's *Death of a Naturalist*,[13] had been discussed by fourth and fifth year groups and it was partly out of curiosity to see how they would respond that it was given to the first years. They began by giggling over the word 'farting' — 'said it as if it was some old ordinary word, you know!' remarked Robert in amazement — but they move rapidly into trying to place the story within the context of the bizarre as they have encountered it: 'Sounds like a thriller,' says Richard, and, a few lines later, 'Sounds like something out of *Dr Who*'. The television reference immediately sparks off comparisons with the previous night's television programme on strange happenings, Arthur C. Clark's *Mysterious World*. All the time this is going on, the conversation is punctuated by individuals murmuring lines over to themselves, re-telling them, savouring them: seven of the first twenty-one utterances are simply individuals trying over particular lines. They respond immediately to the tone of the poem:

30	*Liz*	It's a bit grotty, isn't it?
31	*Rachel*	Yeah.
32	*Liz*	And the slimy spawn.
33	*Philip*	I think it was quite a good poem.
34	*Liz*	Ugh . . . all like jelly.
35	*Mary*	Makes you think of —
36	*Robert*	A brain —
37	*Mary*	Stagnant pools full of water (*savouring it*)
38	*Liz*	Yeah.
39	*Philip*	I think that —
40	*Liz*	And bluebottles going in and out in it. (*Savouring it*)
41	*Philip*	I think it could have been made a bit —
42	*Liz*	Smell . . . slobber . . . (*savouring it*)
43	*Rachel*	Ugh . . . slobber . . . ugh . . . yuk. All together . . .
44	*Philip*	When you think . . . when you said that it reminded me of 'Slime'. I like that: that was that green stuff.

They constantly return, and with evident relish, to the 'strong gauze of sound' that Heaney weaves in his poem, enjoying the shudder it sends through them, perhaps feeling themselves close to forbidden ground:

69	*Mary*	It's a boiling hot day and everything's all smelly —
70	*Liz*	Yeah.
71	*Mary*	And you're all sticky and it's all sweltering and —
72	*Philip*	That's the thing.
73	*Robert*	'One day, when fields were rank —'
74	*Rachel*	Green, thick, slobbery . . . all gooey and . . .

Death of a Naturalist

All year the flax-dam festered in the heart
Of the townland; green and heavy headed
Flax had rotted there, weighted down by huge sods.
Daily it sweltered in the punishing sun.
Bubbles gargled delicately, bluebottles
Wove a strong gauze of sound around the smell.
There were dragon-flies, spotted butterflies,
But best of all was the warm thick slobber
Of frogspawn that grew like clotted water
In the shade of the banks. Here, every spring
I would fill jampotfuls of the jellied
Specks to range on window-sills at home,
On shelves at school, and wait and watch until
The fattening dots burst into nimble –
Swimming tadpoles. Miss Walls would tell us how
The daddy frog was called a bullfrog
And how he croaked and how the mammy frog
Laid hundreds of little eggs and this was
Frogspawn. You could tell the weather by frogs too
For they were yellow in the sun and brown
In rain.

   Then one hot day when fields were rank
With cowdung in the grass the angry frogs
Invaded the flax-dam; I ducked through hedges
To a coarse croaking that I had not heard
Before. The air was thick with a bass chorus.
Right down the dam gross-bellied frogs were cocked
On sods; their loose necks pulsed like sails. Some hopped:
The slap and plop were obscene threats. Some sat
Poised like mud grenades, their blunt heads farting.
I sickened, turned, and ran. The great slime kings
Were gathered there for vengeance and I knew
That if I dipped my hand the spawn would clutch it.

Seamus Heaney

75 *Philip*   But you've got . . . It's like
               sludge with black dots in it . . .

Relating the poem to their own experiences
continues to be a main way of coming to grips
with it. Their memories of playing with 'Slime'
(joke shop variety) are developed quite se-
riously over several exchanges and there is too a
memory of a ghost story 'about this man who
cut up all these frogs and in the end they ate a
hole through him'. There are exchanges about
looking for frogspawn themselves, about
catching newts and lizards. Rachel remembers
an episode with spiders: 'I remember, when I
was little, my brother and his friends, we were
walking down the brook and one of these great
big spiders walked up my leg and I screamed
and they ran out of the brook and left me there
with this spider walking up me.' Robert
remembers catching newts: 'We used to catch
newts mainly. We used to put them on the bank
bit and they used to wade through all this mud
and they used to get back in.' Lisa remembers
being frightened by leeches. Philip recalls looking for a grass snake in his grandma's garden:
'When I saw it I was so paralysed.' All con-
tribute memories related to the central theme of
the poem though again it is Philip and Robert
who come to dominate the later exchanges.
What appears to be happening is characteristic
of much first and second year talk arising from
poems: it is essentially an anecdotal 'paralleling'
of the central experience of the poem which
helps them to 'place' it, to give it meaning
within their own frames of reference and
ultimately to show that, at one level at least,
they 'possess' the poem even if a detailed
analysis of it is beyond their powers.

100 *Robert*   We used to play behind the
                bank and there used to be ant
                hills.
101 *Philip*   These great big ant hills, and
                because of the sun — they take
                up heat these ant hills —
102 *Robert*   — in the sunshine.
103 *Philip*   They're all little grey sand stuff.

104 *Robert*   In the summer it's nice 'cos
                you go round trying to catch
                lizards.
105 *Philip*   These little orange ant things
                build 'em like this — massive —
                they grow quite big and it
                makes . . . brings
                a . . . well . . .
106 *Robert*   Constructs.
107 *Philip*   And it takes all the heat from
                the sun and the lizards like the
                heat and they go out there.
108 *Robert*   Early in the morning they're
                on the stones but they change.
                If we're catching lizards over
                there, we're normally having
                fights — play fights — about ten
                of us against ten. We keep fal-
                ling over the ant hills and
                everything and then all the
                ants start coming out and we
                run like hell!
109 *Rachel*   I think it's really good this
                poem.
110 *Robert*   Some of them are off the
                ground like this and you can't
                see 'em and you go flying and
                some are like this and you run,
                you jump and you catch your
                feet.
111 *Philip*   Yeah, 'cos it's by a railway
                embankment and all up the
                side.
112 *Robert*   Yeah, there's the railway and
                it's got them coming out the
                side down 'ere and we play
                down 'ere. Sometimes you go
                about half way up the bank,
                run down and you knock
                people over and they start run-
                ning away from you and they
                fall over and they kick it and
                it starts coming and all the ants
                come out so they run.
113 *Mary*   Oh, I should —
114 *Liz*   I hate ants.

115 *Philip*   I used to collect ants and I
used to put them in a jar,
shake 'em up and they used to
start killing each other and I
thought that was brilliant.

The story of the frogs and their vengeance is
thus related to their own experience: they
recognise the feelings of guilt and retribution
implicit in their own experience of the natural
world and recall other episodes. Robert remembers 'We had these magnifying glasses and
we found these spiders and one of us held it
down and the other one was burning it with a
magnifying glass.' Philip tells of shaking a fence
post and disturbing a wasps' nest '— and suddenly I heard this buzzing noise and I can't see
anything and then there was all these wasps
coming out. I went "Leg it!"' Later, Philip
recollects 'there's a stagnant pool round where I
live, and it's full of rubbish and sometimes it
stinks in a hot summer — it attracts a lot of
mosquitoes and we've got this bit called the
snake pit 'cos there's tons of long metal
bits . . . in a sort of dip. And if you jump in,
because you move, they all sort of go on top of
you and you go Aagh! Snakes! Snakes!'

This 'paralleling' activity might easily be
dismissed by the casual listener as idle chat but
closer examination shows it to be reflecting
central concerns of the poem and providing a
means of relating it to the kind of knowledge
and experience the children bring with them to
the classroom. A beginning student teacher
once said of these children 'The trouble is, they
don't know anything.' He could not have been
listening. That personal knowledge which
every child brings into the classroom and which
long pre-dates any abstract awareness of poetic
process and technique or of critical method, is
not to be despised and might usefully be
encouraged much further up the school than is
commonly the case. Encouraging and developing an interaction between the work and the
reader at all levels and particularly at the level of
personal meaning-making keeps poetry from

becoming the irrelevant, sterile game remarked
on earlier, the ultimate aim of which may be the
skilful despatch of what Anthony Burgess
appropriately describes as 'anonymous texts
laid out on our desks like preserved frogs for
anatomical probing.'[14] At this stage, the children are more concerned to match the patterns
of experience recounted in the poem with their
own.

We seek patterns all the time: making patterns is the stuff of human perception. That
being so we may follow Robin Skelton's
argument that 'the poem, by being so obviously a pattern, presents . . . an experience
embodying a formal indication of the way in
which all experience is perceived. The poem
not only presents a pattern of experience but
also an experience of pattern itself'.[15] In teasing out or re-enacting the structures of the Hughes'
poem, in seeing the wider implications of *The
Bully Asleep,* in becoming Munro's indulged
cat, or in relating Heaney's childhood memory
to their own experience, the different groups
are engaged in the serious game of pattern
recognition.

In a sense all comprehension implies recognition of patterns and in poetry the constant
interplay between the structural elements —
metrical patterns, patterns of imagery, sound
and syntax, for example — and the elements of
experience brought by creative artist and recreative reader, provides a complex interaction
of overlaid patterns within which we seek
coherence and form. It is the element of
personal   experience   that   shapes   each
individual's poem which he or she conjures
from the text.

* * *

There have been a number of approaches
to the analysis of teacher/class interaction.
Analysis and evaluation of pupil/pupil talk is
yet more difficult and no entirely satisfactory
method has yet been evolved. Wade's somewhat simple designation of categories of utter-
ance[16] when considering small group dis-

cussion of a poem is derived in part from Squire's earlier work on story[17] and although it does not offer the more subtle distinctions and, most important, the 'frames' evolved by Barnes and Todd,[18] it does offer a starting point for considering some aspects of small group conversation.

Wade proposes six categories: Judging, Interpreting, Re-telling, Associating, Explicating and Miscellaneous. His research suggests that pupils working in small groups spend very much more time making judgements or interpretations, re-telling and savouring the words and matching their own experiences to the poem, whereas in a typically teacher directed group by far the greatest number of responses fall into the 'Explicating' category in response to teacher's questioning. The other categories are poorly represented or entirely absent. Experience over a wide range of groups would suggest that whilst it is true that the stress is often very much as Wade found it to be and that, in self-directed groups, 'Explication' is generally a relatively minor part of pupils' response, it may figure much more prominently with older pupils and where the poem is particularly densely packed (e.g. the Hughes poem quoted earlier). In the case of the first year discussion of the Munro poem *Milk for the cat* some 75% of the utterances fall into the Judging, Interpreting, Re-telling, Associating categories, far higher than one might expect from a teacher led discussion; in discussions of *The Warm and the Cold,* the 'Explication' figure has invariably remained high.

Explication, that literal 'unfolding' of the text, is not of less value or importance than these other activities. As we have seen from one of the tapes in particular, it can provide a natural and powerful motivation to engage with the poem, tapping the drive towards order and assimilation and offering the reward of personal satisfaction which fuels further inquiry. It is the driving force behind such explication that is important. If the need to know stems only from outside, from the teacher's direct questions forcing the class over or through the poem as an intellectual obstacle race, then engagement is likely to be superficial at best. If it stems from a sense of discovery and its attendant satisfaction then the readers will more readily make the poem their own.

There is, as we have seen, no one way to approach a poem, no one correct reading, and different poems will call up different aspects of engagement which will themselves vary with different individuals and the singularity of their experience. Operative response, intellectual comprehension, perceptual engagement and evaluative response are all, as D. W. Harding suggests, in a state of 'continuous fusion'.[19] In Rosenblatt's terms there is a continuous shuttling between the *efferent* reading of the poem (i.e. where the reader's attention is focussed primarily upon what will remain as the residue after reading) and the *aesthetic* reading (i.e. where the reader's attention is primarily concerned with what happens during the event and is centred directly on what he is living through during his relationship with that particular text).[20] No one element is easily isolable and for that reason if for no other we should be chary of allocating readers' responses to neat little boxes labelled 'Judgement' or 'Interpretation'. At the very simplest level the task becomes extremely difficult: the 'Miscellaneous' murmur 'mmm', for example, may convey an insight or judgement shared or valued . . . or not. Norman Holland remarked on 'the sameness one reader brings to different stories and the differences different readers bring to the same story'[21] and it may be that his suggestion of there being a 'personal style' in reading where the reader 'rehearses his own psychological make-up irrespective of the text he is reading' has relevance also to poetry, providing yet another complex layer to fuse with the rest.

Research during the 'seventies and these more recent tapes, consistently point to the value of group approaches to poetry at all levels. The survey figures given earlier (see p. 24) indicate that at best around a third of teachers of classes in years one to five would 'always' or 'often' spend some time in discussing poems in small groups; in most year groups the proportion is a quarter or less. Up to about half the teachers of first year classes 'rarely' or 'never' spend any time on the activity. It may be remembered that in the analysis of 184 lessions across the five year groups only between 5 % and 9 % contained an element of small group discussion. It appears that, despite the research evidence in its favour, small group discussion in this context at least is still relatively uncommon.

Although the tape-recording of groups is by no means essential for the success of small group work and indeed is not practicable for much of the time, it is worth using the tape recorder on a regular basis as a teaching rather than a research tool. Such taped group work may well take place when the remainder of the class is either engaged in parallel non-taped groups or whole class discussion of the same piece. As suggested above, comparison of the kinds of talk that go on in each type of discussion can be very revealing to the teacher.

The next stage in the process may well be to offer pupils the opportunity to listen to and comment on their discussion. (Best of all is to present them with a transcript but it is not realistic to expect the busy class teacher to be able to do this.) Initially, self-consciousness on the part of children hearing their own voices on tape may present something of a barrier but this will generally disappear fairly quickly as they become engrossed in what they have said. It is not uncommon to find groups excited, even impressed by their own words and individuals will frequently offer further amplification of comments made . . . 'No, when I said that what I *really* meant was . . .' They need a copy of the poem to hand when doing this and may well find themselves going even deeper into the poem as a result. It is, of course, perfectly possible to tape-record this discussion of a discussion. Quite where the progression might stop is impossible to say — it has some similarities with the effect produced by looking

down the endless succession of reflections seen when two mirrors face each other — but practical considerations preclude further experiment! The key to the success of the enterprise must be that pupils are not put in the position of feeling that their talk is being evaluated; always, in whatever context, the message must be that it is valued and that talking in this way is a worthwhile activity.

Individuals within groups will recognise their differences and may or may not find agreement, even something approaching consensus within their group. Whether they do so or not does not matter: consensus is not the aim of their talk. When a whole class is working in small groups it is sometimes helpful to give each pupil a personal investment in the poem by asking for a brief, concentrated jotting down of first impressions as outlined below before launching them into group talk. Sometimes it is appropriate to appoint a group secretary to report back. Eventually the aim is to widen discussion between groups, developing the network from the tentativeness of the individual's 'I think . . .' uttered in the security of the small group, to the relative assertiveness perhaps of the group's 'We think . . .' and back, if the talk goes well, to the individual's 'I think . . .' uttered this time with greater assurance. Whatever method is adopted it is essential to leave time at the end for the poem to be read aloud once again and for it to be read well. 'We murder to dissect' and if the poem is left in its component parts at the end of such a session and not reassembled and experienced in the light of the new individual and collective insights of the group or class then we have lost sight of the central aim of the activity.

The lightly structured, self-directed discussion, whether taped or not, has great value in the way in which it offers an open-ended approach to what is often seen as a somewhat forbidding, even alien task. It appears to be a key activity in the demystification of poetry or, more accurately, in the demystification of attitudes towards poetry. If pupils can be brought to see how the discourse of poetry is achieved, how it works to certain ends, indeed that 'cleverness' remarked earlier which is rooted in the poet's craft, that understanding may lead to delight. It isn't the only route but it is an important one for some readers and for some poems.

Small group discussion should not be seen as a panacea though it could usefully be treated with less caution or suspicion than is commonly the case. Some attendant difficulties have been noted earlier (p. 46) and practising teachers will not be slow to add their own problems to the list. Such drawbacks are rarely insuperable however and it seems regrettable that we are not yet making greater use of what is clearly a most valuable tool for both teaching and learning. The move is away from the essentially 'pyramidical' structure of exchange in most lessons with the teacher as the focus, soliciting,

receiving, interpreting, assessing and legitimising contributions and dispensing knowledge. We aim instead to create a 'network' model, not simply for all the oft-quoted benefits of small group work, but because it is an outward and visible sign of a willingness to recognise and value the diversity of interpretation and experience pupils may bring to a poem and a challenge to the view that there is a single 'correct' interpretation of any piece to which we should aspire.

Poetry, good poetry, is robust stuff and will endure rougher treatment than it is sometimes allowed. At times Raymond O'Malley's complaint that 'there has been too much raucous handling' of poetry may seem to be just but in the final analysis, it is perhaps better that it is handled, however roughly, than set apart as a sacred mystery never to be touched and, in consequence maybe, never to touch our pupils.

CHAPTER FIVE

Talking About Poetry — Other Approaches

'*I* can repeat poetry as well as other folk if it comes to that—'

'Oh, it needn't come to that!' Alice hastily said.

(*Through the Looking-Glass*, Chapter 6)

Clearly self-directed discussion is by no means the answer to all difficulties in the teaching of poetry and the effects of other groups' contributions and of the teacher's participation at a later stage in the lesson are not to be underestimated. At some point in opening up the discourse of poetry it may be important to introduce a more structured approach to reading a poem. The problem in doing so is that either overtly or by implication the teacher runs the risk of suggesting that a 'true meaning' is there to be found, that there is only one acceptable reading, that finally, the teacher retains a monopoly over that truth rather after the fashion of the college professor described by H. G. Wells: 'He was one of those who teach us how to appreciate poetry and prose, and when to say Oh! and Ah! and when to shake one's head about it discouragingly, like a bus conductor who is proffered a doubtful coin.' Nearer home, the third year pupils perceive the problems thus:

596	Graham	. . . This has taken us about half an hour to think about this, hasn't it?
597	Tom	Yeah.
598	Graham	So in class we wouldn't have that long.
599	Zoe	We wouldn't have half an hour, no . . .
600	Nick	No we'd have about five minutes then the teacher would tell us what we're thinking about it.
601	Graham	But, yeah, the teacher would tell us —
602	Zoe	— try and tell us, try and tell us.
603	Graham	— What we should say this, this, this poem is on about and then she'd ask you for your own ideas and to write something in your rough book about it and you wouldn't know what you were on about.
604	Tom	Yeah and she'd say 'Do you

agree with me?' and if you say 'No' she'd say (*mimics exasperated teacherly voice*) 'Well what do you bloody think then?' (*Laughter*) and you'd have to . . . she'd have a . . .

605   *Zoe*   You'd end up in front of everybody else . . .

Lack of time, lack of direction, insistence on a 'correct' interpretation, public exposure of pupils' almost inevitably 'inadequate' grasp of the poem in these circumstances can only lead to uncertainty and mistrust when faced with poems in class. With such caveats in mind, any more directive, structured approach to poetry is likely to look somewhat mechanistic and reminiscent of 'practical criticism' when presented for inspection on the page. Nonetheless the attempt should be made.

Perhaps the most problematic area identified in the course of the survey quoted earlier was that of moving away from simple reading for pleasure with younger classes to reading in depth with public examinations in view. Strategies adopted were various but tended to rely in large measure on teacher explication, and rarely offered opportunity for personal engagement or commitment to the poem. The outline of activities offered here is designed to allow for both independent thought and group discussion within a structured framework. It is emphatically not directive in that it remains open-ended and is only suggestive of a 'way in': it can certainly be added to or shortened or simplified by individual teachers. Most usefully perhaps, it can be used as a common starting point for both teacher and pupils and the teacher may undertake the task alongside them.

For those teachers who do not find technology too daunting or gimmicky, a fascinating way of sharing their own responses with those of the class is to jot their own notes on a previously prepared overhead projector (OHP) transparency of the poem. Pupils' own insights — often as perceptive as the teacher's —

can be added when whole class discussion takes place or, more helpfully, the class's notes can be collected first on to the transparency and the teacher's then added or compared. The immediacy of this approach and the genuinely open, collaborative nature of the experience make it a valuable teaching strategy. It is offered here in the form in which it might finally be presented to a class but in practice individual aspects of it would first be singled out and talked through by the teacher. Without such mediation it is likely to prove too daunting.

Group work on a poem

You can use the suggestions below as a 'way in' to a poem working either on your own or as a member of a group. You will probably find a group approach most helpful — certainly so at first.

If you are working in a group you may find that it makes for more lively discussion if two or three of you move from A to B to C (all the suggestions in B start with how the language of the poem works) and for two or three to move from A to C to B (the suggestions in C start mainly with feelings). Language and feelings cannot really be separated in this way, as you will soon find once you begin to talk, but coming at it from two slightly different directions can help to start you thinking.

Remember, these are only suggestions: you can add to them or shorten them. Some of the ideas will not be much use with some poems. Laid out on the page like this it looks rather a lot to take in and seems all too neat and tidy. Do not worry about it: after using the ideas as a starting point a few times you will find that you do not need to refer to them very often.

A

In groups, if possible, listen to the poem read aloud.

On your own and without discussion, jot down any ideas that come to mind immediately after the first reading. Spend no more than 4–5 minutes on this. Don't concern yourselves with 'meaning', concentrate on anything that the poem may remind you of, any feelings, however unexpected, it suggests, any kind of atmosphere. There may be nothing: it doesn't matter.

B

Read the poem over to yourselves again – aloud if possible so that you hear it. One member of the group could read the poem or you could share the lines or verses between you. As a group, if possible, underline or circle ideas that occur to you when you ask the following questions. Some people find it very helpful to make notes on the text and jottings in the margin: if you can't do this, a sheet of paper alongside the poem will serve. Share your ideas as a group and talk your way through them after a while:

(i) Which lines or images did you like or find particularly striking or strange even if you didn't quite understand them?

(ii) Jot down one or two questions about the poem that you would like answered.

(iii) Look at the poem on the page – at arm's length if you like – what do you notice about its appearance? What is its shape? Regular verses? a short single block? sprawling across the page? short lines? long lines? Anything else? The writer decided to present the poem in this way: are there any obvious reasons for that decision?

(iv) Look more closely. Is it written in a form you recognise such as a haiku, free verse, rhymed verse, syllabic verse, a ballad, a sonnet . . . ? It's quite possible that you will not recognise a form and it is really not all that important that you should.

(v) Ring round or note anything that seems to form a pattern. It might be a line or a word or an idea that is repeated from time to time. It might be a sound that is repeated or a mental picture that recurs. There may be comparisons (similes or metaphors) that are repeated. Are any such ideas or images linked or developed in any way?

(vi) What do you notice about the language of the poem? Is there a frequent use of adjectives, adverbs – if so, do they have any common theme? Is the poem written in the past, present or future tense? Does it change at any point?

(vii) How does the poem seem to 'move'? Does the sound and rhythm of the lines seem light and bubbly, for example, or do the lines move slowly with heavy rounded sounds and a slow rhythm? Is it different at different places in the poem? Does the punctuation, or lack of it, help you to see how it might be read? Do the lines run on into each other without a break, for example, or are their ends sharply marked by punctuation? Try parts of it out by saying them aloud and listening.

C

Read the poem through again and try to think of words that suggest the *mood* of the piece. Does it feel happy, sad, sentimental, defiant, thoughtful, triumphant, unemotional . . . etc.? On your own, jot down the words you think of. Compare yours with those jotted by others in the group. Talk about why you made the choices you did.

(i) Does the poem seem to develop a line of argument? (e.g. one line might start with the word 'If . .' and further down there might be a line beginning 'Then . .' or 'So . .' or 'But . .' all words that might advance an argument). Does it move to a conclusion, a particular point of view at the end? Note any key words in the development of such a line of thought.

(ii) Is it the poet's voice speaking in the poem

or is it the voice of somebody else, real or imagined?

(iii) Is the poet speaking out to you? quietly reflecting to himself/herself? addressing the world in general . . . . ? If there is another voice in the poem, is it doing the same?

(iv) How does the poet feel about you, the reader? Are you being asked to share something almost personal? Are you being pleaded with? mocked or laughed at? preached at? Is the poet trying to teach you? persuade you? move you? entertain you? . . . something else? How do you know this?

(v) How does the poet feel about the subject of the poem? Are you being offered a message or a view of things that the writer wants you to share or understand? If so, think about why this might be. Does the poem's title suggest anything about the writer's feelings?

D

(i) Look back at your first notes where you jotted down questions you wanted answering. Have you found answers now? If not, can anyone in the group help?

(ii) Read the poem again in the light of your thoughts and notes. Make any further jottings. Relax. Read it again.

Given such a framework, the last thing any class should be asked to do is to work through it slavishly whatever piece is before them. Some of the suggested points for discussion will be inappropriate for some poems and for some circumstances. What is offered is a checklist which within a short time can be largely internalised and, in practice, becomes far less mechanistic than it appears when laid out on the page. The individual teacher may choose to adapt or modify it in the light of his class's needs and abilities and the appropriateness of the guidelines to the poem under discussion. Experience indicates that some such framework often gives direction where it was lacking and is

not only welcomed by pupils as a means of sharpening and ordering their ideas about a poem, but also as deepening their enjoyment.

Jotting down ideas in this way helps pupils over the first hurdle, invites commitment, allows them to open up areas of difficulty unself-consciously and offers common ground for talk to take place. One example of such jotting from a boy in his first term in the sixth is offered alongside my own version as I quite genuinely tackled the poem for the first time. It is important to realise that we both of us saw many similar things but that we also responded to different ones. I had been much concerned with images of death lurking beneath the poem's surface: he had not. He, on the other hand, had been very conscious of the strong foregrounding of the senses: I hadn't. My subsequent reading was enriched by his perceptions.

The above strategy for approaching a poem suggests two parallel lines of thought – one concerned with language, the other with sentiment – though, in practice this is an impossible distinction to sustain. Although it may be helpful to concentrate on particular aspects of the poem – sound, imagery, rhyme, rhythm, form etc. – none of these exists in isolation and they interact in such a way as to define and focus the experience. A poem is, as the word suggests, something *made*, a verbal construct and as such may be deconstructed but we should not lose sight of the fact that its particular sense of *wholeness* may carry us through the problems posed by individual lines or images which we find initially, in some cases ultimately, difficult to grasp. Trusting the poem, especially for the young or inexperienced reader, is not always easy and it may be helpful to bear in mind I. A. Richards' advice on tackling a difficult text: 'Read it as though it made sense'.[1] Ideas, patterns, associations often begin to emerge if we do this; things that may remain out of reach if the poem is approached in linear fashion as a sequence of hurdles to be jumped with 'the real meaning' of the poem as the prize at the finish.

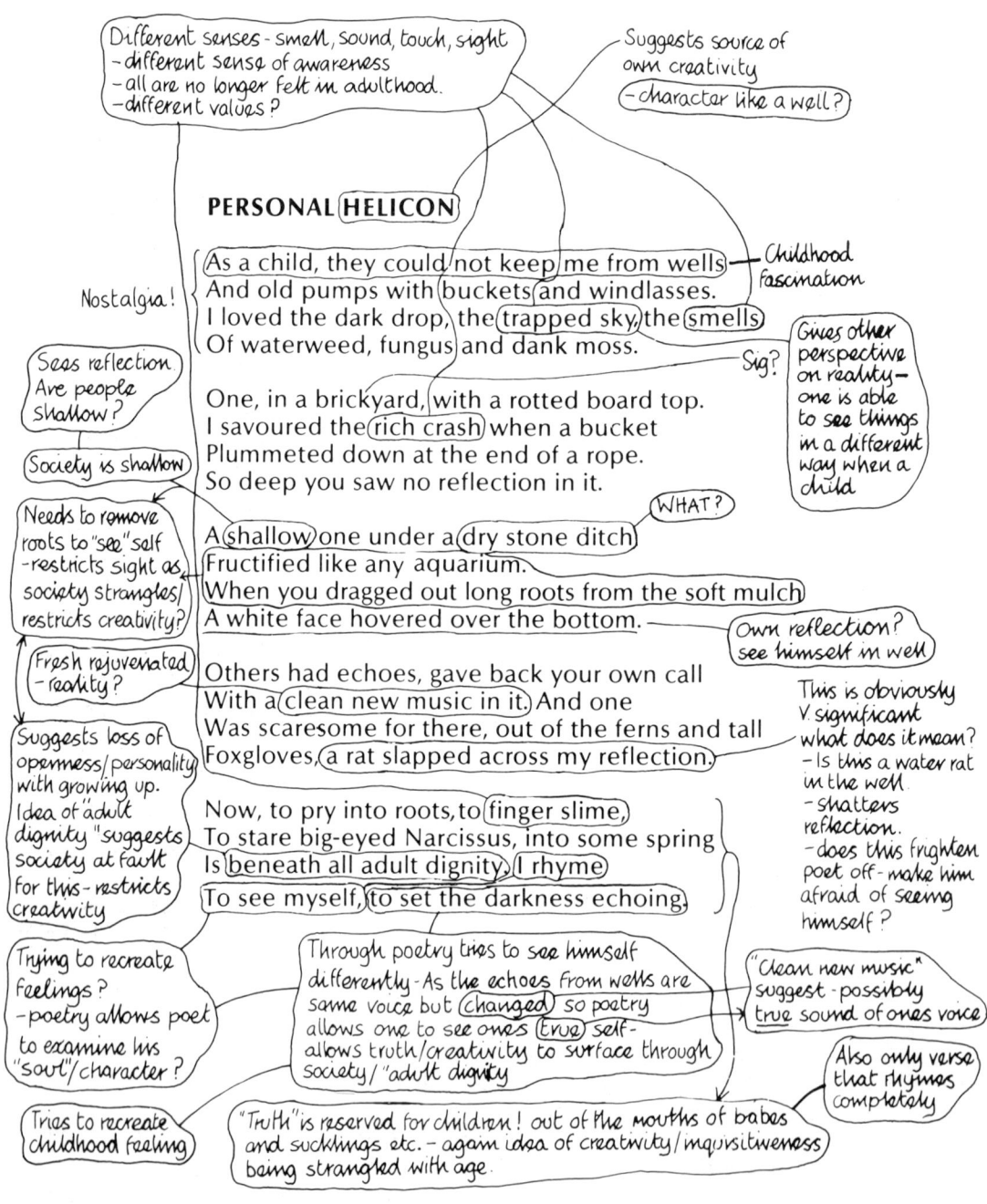

Different senses - smell, sound, touch, sight
- different sense of awareness
- all are no longer felt in adulthood.
- different values?

Suggests source of own creativity
(- character like a well?)

PERSONAL HELICON

As a child, they could not keep me from wells ── Childhood fascination
And old pumps with buckets and windlasses.
I loved the dark drop, the trapped sky, the smells
Of waterweed, fungus and dank moss.

Nostalgia!

Seas reflection Are people shallow?

Society is shallow

Needs to remove roots to "see" self - restricts sight as, society strangles/ restricts creativity?

Fresh rejuvenated - reality?

One, in a brickyard, with a rotted board top.
I savoured the rich crash when a bucket
Plummeted down at the end of a rope.
So deep you saw no reflection in it.

Sig?

Gives other perspective on reality— one is able to see things in a different way when a child

WHAT?

A shallow one under a dry stone ditch
Fructified like any aquarium.
When you dragged out long roots from the soft mulch
A white face hovered over the bottom. ──

Own reflection? see himself in well

Others had echoes, gave back your own call
With a clean new music in it. And one
Was scaresome for there, out of the ferns and tall
Foxgloves, a rat slapped across my reflection.

This is obviously V. significant what does it mean?
- Is this a water rat in the well
- shatters reflection.
- does this frighten poet off - make him afraid of seeing himself?

Suggests loss of openness/ personality with growing up. Idea of "adult dignity" suggests society at fault for this - restricts creativity

Now, to pry into roots, to finger slime,
To stare big-eyed Narcissus, into some spring
Is beneath all adult dignity, I rhyme
To see myself, to set the darkness echoing.

Trying to recreate feelings?
- poetry allows poet to examine his "soul"/character?

Through poetry tries to see himself differently - As the echoes from wells are same voice but changed so poetry allows one to see ones true self - allows truth/creativity to surface through society/ "adult dignity"

"Clean new music" suggest - possibly true sound of ones voice

Also only verse that rhymes completely

Tries to recreate childhood feeling

"Truth" is reserved for children! out of the mouths of babes and sucklings etc. - again idea of creativity/ inquisitiveness being strangled with age.

Boy: 1st term in 6th form

PERSONAL HELICON

*Springs oa Mt. Helicon
Sacred to Muses*

*Held together by
a,b,a,b half
rhyme. Note
stresses??
10 syllables*

As a child, they could not keep me from <u>wells</u>
And old pumps with buckets and windlasses.
I loved the dark drop, the trapped sky, the smells
Of waterweed, fungus and dank <u>moss.</u>   ①

*Conversational Tone
Easy & Relaxed as
though beginning
a story*

Immediate & precise

*Images continue
with 'rotted',
'savoured', 'rich'
strong, full vowel
sounds 'echo sense
of strong
satisfaction.*

One, in a brickyard, with a rotted board top.
I s<u>av</u>oured the <u>rich</u> cr<u>ash</u> when a bucket
Plummeted d<u>ow</u>n at the end of a rope.
So deep you saw no reflection in it.   ②

*Pleasure /? Fascination
in darkness, trapped,
smells, weed fungus
? Pre-occupation with
death? Are there echoes
of the hangman's trap
door ('dark drop', 'rotted
boardtop,' 'plummeted)*

*suggests 'feeling
with life'*

*Tactile, long lined
echoes movement.*

A shallow one under a dry stone ditch
Fructified like any aquarium.
When you dragged out long roots from the soft mulch
A white face hovered over the bottom.   ③

*? Stress on life
here but only
in the shallow
one.*

*repeated hard,
bright consonants
suggest clearness
clarity in contrast
to soft vowel
sounds elsewhere*

Others had e<u>ch</u>oes, gave ba<u>ck</u> your own <u>call</u>
With a <u>cl</u>ean new musi<u>c</u> in it. And one
Was s<u>c</u>aresome (for there, out of the ferns and tall
Foxgloves, a rat slapped across my reflection.   ④

*Own face but suggests
suicide's face too? This
is where he finds himself?
Root His roots?
Again finding self but
in a positive way.
Suggests 'own voice'
as a poet*

*Soft alliteration
helps build quiet
mood before
harsh / short
Sound shatters it.*

Now, to pry into roots to finger slime,
To stare big-eyed <u>Narcissus</u>, into some spring
Is beneath all adult dignity. I rhyme
To see my<u>s</u>elf, to set the darkness echoing.

*Powerful, short sharp sound
re-enacts the sudden shock.
⑤ Feed image of death.
Again. Roots both real and
symbolic?*

*cf (sight).
reflection in water*   *(sound)*

*(Echoes Helicon)
Self-regarding · Looking
into self.*

*So does every
verse ①–⑤
with images
of darkness
& maybe
suggestive of
death.*

*The poems become 'wells' into himself
He lightly mocks himself. Brings us
back to the opening & clinches the poem.
Ends as it began - in the darkness. There
is pleasure but fear is now, as then,
present (? predominant) An amused panic
on the surface, deeper fear lies beneath.
We are literally concerned with the springs of
his poetry as well as figuratively.*

*N.B. These are
the only full
rhymes.*

Cleanth Brooks and Robert Penn Warren rightly warn against seeing poetry as 'a bundle of things that are "poetic" in themselves' or as 'a kind of box, decorated or not, in which a "truth" or a "fine sentiment" is hidden', or as 'a group of mechanically combined elements' of metre, rhyme etc. and they too stress the particular wholeness of poems:

> The poem, in its vital unity, is a 'formed' thing, a thing existing in itself, and its vital unity, its form, embodies — *is* — its meaning. Yet paradoxically, by *the fact of its being 'formed' and having its special identity, it somehow makes us more aware of the life outside itself.* By its own significance it awakens us to the significance of our own experience of the world.[2]

The sense of 'vital unity' of 'completeness' is, of course, achieved in large measure deliberately, by making certain choices and by exclusion as well as inclusion. We can usefully ask what ideas or associations that we might have expected to find are *not* treated in the poem? Why was this form chosen in preference to others? Why this tone rather than another? Why this image? What other possibilities can you envisage? Why the exclusion of those possibilities? What might have been the effect of including them? Of course such observations are highly speculative but there is a sense in which by defining what a piece *is not* we come closer to understanding what it *is*. The decisions, both conscious and unconscious, that shape a piece and give the chosen form its particularity can be revealing.

* * *

There are a number of ways in which classes may be encouraged to talk about poems without writing being the unvarying outcome. Apart from small group talk of the kind already discussed where taping may or may not form part of the exercise, the following approaches have been found to work well with pupils across the age range.

Prepared reading

The 'party piece' prepared and presented by the individual pupil has some value perhaps in certain contexts but the drawbacks — a tendency for one or two children to dominate, overly self-conscious 'elocution', lack of interest from the rest of the class whilst each individual performs, the time needed, the resistance of not a few children to this kind of exposure, the fact that it is the performance not the poem which is the main object — suggest that it is not the best way of approaching a prepared reading.

Instead a poem may be taken up by small groups as a result either of group choice or direction by the teacher and the groups asked to discuss it and prepare a reading. Depending on the nature of the poem and the groups' interpretation of it, such a reading may be a joint effort with lines or verses distributed, it may be a choral reading, it may be presented by just one or two of the group. Although the presentation is important, just as important is the preceding discussion on how each group feels the poem might best be read. Inevitably such talk quickly takes them into discussing the meaning of lines, interpreting tone and attitude, the structure of the poem and other features. There is an end product to work towards and a sense of positive engagement from most pupils.

If it is possible, provide tape-recorders: it is striking how groups will re-work their reading several times in order to produce the best version. Once the initial self-consciousness has worn off, groups frequently settle into a very professional style of working and, listening to their conversation, it is often evident that they are capable not only engaging with poems in this way but of being productively self-critical. The way in which one of the third year groups whose conversation was monitored earlier chose to engage with a poem is an example of the kind of understanding group reading can bring about. Presentation of prepared reading of this kind can lead into full class discussion of a piece: one in which all now have some sort of personal stake, some commitment.

Choral speaking

Choral speaking of verse is one of the possible outcomes of the above suggestion and it also has merit in its own right as an enjoyable and stimulating way of engaging children more deeply in poetry. It is a pity that in recent years, partly because of an over-emphasis on elocution rather than on enjoyment, this approach has been out of fashion. Pairs, small groups, whole classes can be encouraged to experiment with choral or group presentations which, apart from the advantages outlined above, help children, quite unconsciously, develop an ear for the rhythm, sound and movement of lines: concepts which if presented abstractly rather than being experienced actively, would for many remain dull and irrelevant. Developing an ear for how a poem might be read helps them develop the ability to hear lines in the head and to test them on the inner ear.

Many poems lend themselves to interpretation by two or more voices. Highly successful pieces have been several poems by Brian Lee, particularly his *Words*, Henry Treece's *The Magic Wood*, any number of Michael Rosen's poems such as *I'm The Youngest in Our House*, Ted Hughes' *Leaves*, Charles Causley's *Mary, Mary Magdalene* and many of his ballads, 'sound' poems such as Eleanor Farjeon's *Cat*, Edwin Morgan's *Off Course*, *The Loch Ness Monster's Song* etc., George Macbeth's lengthy poem *Noah's Journey*, Frank O'Hara's *A True Account of Talking to the Sun at Fire Island* . . . There is an understandable tendency for teachers to be wary of such approaches with students higher up the school but, even at this

level, much can be gained from using two or more voices to interpret some poems. Striking readings of Auden's *As I Walked Out* and C. P. Cavafy's *Waiting For The Barbarians* come to mind, as does a poignant reading of Sylvia Plath's *Metaphors* read line by line using nine girls' voices and a quietly, creepily insistent reading of her poem *Mushrooms* by a group of six fifth year pupils.

Group anthology

This involves the collection and presentation by small groups of an anthology of poems based on the work of a particular poet or on a particular theme. As in the suggestion given above, tape-recording is not necessary but it can be very helpful as a means of focussing groups on the task and giving them an end product to work towards. A time limit of, say, ten minutes should be set for the performance of the finished anthology and as many sources of material as possible should be provided for browsing. As before, this preparatory part of the process, this familiarisation with poems, is in many ways more important than the final outcome. It takes them deeper into the range and experience of poetry in a non-threatening and constructive way.

There is no reason why pupils' own pieces should not be mixed with poems by published authors in this context. Where an introduction to the work of a particular poet is concerned, comments and link passages can be included: where the collection centres round a theme, pupils' own poems may be read. Work that stemmed originally from *Under Milk Wood* developed into a parallel exercise on portraying a school day in verse from waking up, rushed breakfast and journey to school, through calling the register and assembly, to poems about various lessons, school dinners, games, messing about with friends, homework and bed. The most ambitious of these included simple sound effects such as school bells, the sound of classes in corridors, the calling of the register, the recitation of verbs, the echoing bareness of the school gym. It is, in fact, often helpful to suggest that the anthology is presented as though it were a radio broadcast. For the more ambitious, tape – slide presentations or even videos are possibilities.

Other successful collections of this kind have included one on Childhood which stemmed originally from David Holbrook's suggestions in *Thieves and Angels*[3] but developed into a less rosy view of life as it moved from nursery rhymes and Walter de la Mare, to poems by Mike Rosen, Charles Causley, Blake, Roger McGough and themselves. The possibilities are clearly endless and the groups can be organised to work on separate themes, in parallel or, if it is a large project (*The Seven Ages* comes to mind) on sequential parts of it.

One advantage of this kind of project that should be seized upon is that it offers the opportunity to present poetry for an audience other than the class teacher. It can in fact offer a public platform for it and it restores the sense of performance so often missing from children's experience of poetry. The tape or performance for the whole class or for a younger year group, even for children in the local primary school, the performance at an assembly or an open day are all active *celebrations* of poetry.

Poetry and video

Teachers and pupils increasingly have access to video cameras as well as to VCRs and can easily make their own remarkably professional short videotapes. The simplest method of presenting poems in this way is to film the subject – a sleeping cat, a townscape, traffic passing by, a lively playground – and then to dub appropriate poems as 'voice over' afterwards. Videotape allows you to have as many attempts at getting the reading right as you need without destroying the picture. One group of poorly motivated fifth year students

were fired by this approach and produced some excellent material, some of it written by themselves. The matching of visual images and words on the page and the subsequent discussion on how the poem should be read, plus the fact that they can go on improving their reading and that nothing need be final, may take them deep into the poem. An interesting development as a result of the home video boom of recent years – at the latest count over 15 % of British homes had a video recorder – is that pupils will ask if they can take their tape home to show parents and friends.

Cloze deletion

Cloze deletion where specific lexical items are blanked out from a poem (e.g. all the adjectives or all the verbs) has the merit of encouraging talk about the appropriateness of the language and provokes some fierce argument. It is quite possible that pupils will prefer their own version to the original when all is revealed; and, of course, they may be right to do so. This exercise encourages very close attention to the text and demands that they think about the tone and style of the writing as well as technical points such as stress, rhyme and metre. Working in groups, arguing their case for or against a particular choice of word within the group and then as a group before the rest of the class is a lively and productive way of developing awareness of how some aspects of poetry work. It is vitally important, however, to ensure that, after the talk has died down and everyone has had their say, the poem is put back together again and read in its entirety. One quick and useful way of presenting this activity and focussing the class without recourse to lots of paper is to use two OHP transparencies, one with the blanks and one with the missing words. The two are shown together at the end.

At the risk of provoking terminal apoplexy in those for whom all such approaches are sacrilegious, it is suggested that what is perhaps the ultimate cloze, the Microelectronics Education Programme (MEP) computer program known as the *Developing Tray (Tray* for short) is well worth experimenting with.[4] A useful article by Heather Govier, explaining the approach and showing it in use with a group of pupils working on May Swenson's poem *Southbound on the Freeway*, appears in *Acorn User*.[5] Briefly, it involves presenting a small group of children with an incomplete poem on screen (the incompleteness may vary from nothing but punctuation marks to a skeleton version of the poem) and asking them to predict what letters, complete words or phrases correctly fill the blanks. The computer obediently and instantly rewards them by entering correct predictions on the display and adding to their score.

'Sounds appalling . . . ghastly . . .' have been some of the kinder responses from colleagues to whom the program has been outlined. Those who have stayed to try their hand have invariably been hooked. I have found children fascinated and willing to talk through break and lunchtime about what words would or would not be appropriate in the blanks. Tape-recordings of their discussions reveal careful thought about the kind of language used and a growing sensitivity to the tone and structure of the piece. It is, of course, one of the rules of the game that all the group must agree on each decision. Conversations with teachers indicate that many would be horrified to see Frost's delicate and reflective *Stopping by Woods* subjected to this treatment but I must confess to having done it and to being impressed by the level of talk that was achieved and sustained by pupils. Their excitement as they saw the poem taking shape, developing like a photographic negative in its tray, was undeniable.

Sequencing

Sequencing involves presenting pairs or small groups with the lines of a poem 'cut up' either line by line or in larger sense units and asking them to arrange them in what seems to them to be a meaningful order. Some will be able to recreate the original, some will find that they produce a version that they find satisfying though it is not the 'correct' one. Once again, the discussion that takes place as the task is undertaken and the quality of the talk about the acceptability or otherwise of new versions is the measure of the success of the exercise. Again there is every encouragement to look closely at how poems are put together. Three short poems used in this way have been Edward Thomas's *Cock-Crow* and the two well known *Eagle* poems, one by Tennyson and the other by Andrew Young. An example is offered on the next page. It helps to be given a clue about the arrangement of verses but skilled readers will not need that . . .

Draft versions

Offering a writer's early draft versions of poems to a class for comment and discussion has long been a more 'respectable' version of some of the above though it is perhaps surprising to find how rarely teachers actually do it. The successive drafts of Owen's *Anthem for Doomed Youth* must be the best known. Here are the first four lines of the first and fourth drafts with Sassoon's emendations. Copies of the full manuscript texts can be found in *Touchstones 4*.[6] Other examples of writer's work in draft will be found in *Considering Poetry*[7] edited by Brian Phythian and in *Understanding Poetry*[8] by Brooks and Warren (p. 464ff) which includes, amongst others, drafts of poems by Randell Jarrell and by Housman and that splendidly hard-won second stanza of Keats' *Ode To Autumn* which includes the altogether unmemorable

Dosed with read poppies; while thy
    reeping hook
Spares from Some slumbrous
    minutes while the wam slumpers
    creep

The Eagle

Round the hill-side,

Scanning the ground to kill.

He looks as though from his own wings

He hangs between his wings outspread

And bends a narrow golden head,

Level and still

He hung down crucified.

Yet as he sails and smoothly swings

Ringed with the azure world, he stands.

Close to the sun in lonely lands,

And like a thunderbolt he falls.

He watches from his mountain walls,

He clasps the crag with hookéd hands;

The wrinkled sea beneath him crawls;

```
          ANTHEM  FOR  DEAD  YOUTH
       passing
What minute bells for these who die so fast?


          solemn            the
- Only the monstrous anger of our guns


          blind insolence      iron
Let the majestic insults of their iron mouths


          requiem
Be as the priest-words of their burials
                          requiem
                              (first draft)


               *****

              DOOMED
     ANTHEM  FOR  DEAD  YOUTH

What passing-bells for these who die as cattle?
    -Only the monstrous anger of the guns
    Only the stuttering rifles' rapid rattle
Can patter out their hasty orisons.

                    (fourth draft)
```

Presenting poems in draft, particularly in manuscript form, can be enormously helpful in making them accessible. The words printed formally on the page are seen to have an individual behind them, one who consciously shapes the work, who makes mistakes and false starts, who is capable of rather bad lines at times, who even makes spelling mistakes and who may not be above accepting help from others. This 'humanising' of the writing process, relating it to their own imaginative writing is clearly of value, not least because it suggests that poems are not inspirational, sacred objects that cannot be handled. It is another step in the process of de-mystification.

In most of the activities outlined above the 'game' element is important, talk is central, the grading of product non-existent and concentration on the language and structure of verse considerable and freely given. It may be objected that such approaches are destructive of poetry, mechanistic and incontestably not the way in which verse was ever meant to be approached. Work with students of all ages convinces me that the advantages outweigh the problems. The students' sense of relief at being offered a challenging but absorbing 'game' in which all can take part rather than a solemn explication by the teacher is apparent. The realisation that the piece has form, pattern, often a tightly organised structure that they can reveal for themselves, impresses and pleases them. The discovery that their own ideas are not only sought but may be acceptable is particularly satisfying — much more so than the somewhat narrower interpretations either explicitly or implicitly demanded by the traditional 'comprehension' exercise. In all of the above activities, what would traditionally be regarded as 'mistakes' are free from censure and become part of an absorbing learning experience. The co-operative discussion and testing of hypotheses can take place at the simple 'word-spotting' level or at much deeper levels of meaning-making: my experience has been that the one may give pupils sufficient confidence to move into the other. Of course, such approaches should never form the pupils' sole experience of poetry but, presented as part of a wide and lively programme of poetry teaching, they can be a most effective way of helping pupils gain confidence and insight through a familiarity with texts that conventional teaching approaches alone may often deny them.

* * *

A note on the writing of poetry

In the course of this book I have chosen to focus very little on suggestions to develop pupils' own writing of poetry although I do feel it to be a central concern. The reasons for shifting the focus are threefold. Firstly, in conjunction with my brother, Michael Benton, I have in the course of the five volume *Touchstones* series, in the three volumes of *Watchwords* and in *Poetry Workshop*[9] outlined many approaches to the writing of poetry and feel that in terms of practical hints there is little I would wish to add; secondly, there exist many other useful and some excellent books devoted to the writing of poetry in school — Ted Hughes' classic *Poetry In The Making*[10] and Sandy Brownjohn's two eminently practical books *Does It Have To Rhyme?* and *What Rhymes with Secret?*[11] would be outstanding examples; thirdly, and most importantly, the argument of this book is that it is of crucial importance to redress the balance of talk and writing in our teaching of poetry and to restore *activity other than writing*, such as reading widely for enjoyment, small group talk and performance of poetry, to a central position.

This is emphatically not to suggest that pupils' own writing is of less importance. I would subscribe wholeheartedly to the view expressed by Robert Witkin that 'Appreciation need not only be relevant to the mental life of the child but it needs also to be integrated with his expressive activity. Creative reading should not be divorced from creative writing and creative speaking.' The evidence does suggest that we may be too often concerned with obtaining written 'product' of whatever kind, that this can distort our own teaching and pupils' experience of poetry and that it is certainly the cause of much unhappiness amongst teachers. It suggests further that opportunities for creative reading and creative speaking are lacking and that an increasingly narrow experience of poetry is common. If pupils and teachers alike are to be able to handle poetry with delight and with confidence, there needs to be far wider experience of it at all levels based on the pleasure and delight it can give and without the nagging sense that one has to be an 'initiate' either as critic or writer in order to make something of it. We need to do these things if we are to preserve, as I believe we can, the wondering tone of Philip, the first year boy quoted earlier, as he made the discovery that 'The more you speak about it the better it seems to be.'

References

Chapter 1

1 Reeves, J. (1958) *Teaching Poetry*: Heinemann
2 Langdon, M. (1961) *Let the Children Write*, An Explanation of Intensive Writing: Longman
Marshall, S. (1963) *An Experiment in Education*: Cambridge University Press
Clegg, A. B. (1964) *The Excitement of Writing*: Chatto & Windus
Holbrook, D. (1961) *English For Maturity*: Cambridge University Press
Holbrook, D. (1967) *Children's Writing*: Cambridge University Press
3 Reeves, J. (1958) *Op. Cit.*
4 Holbrook, D. *Iron, Honey, Gold*: Cambridge University Press
Summerfield, G. (1967) *Voices*: Penguin Books
Benton, M. G. and Benton, P. (1967–71) *Touchstones 1–5*: Hodder & Stoughton
Williams, E. (1972) *Dragonsteeth*: Arnold
5 Hughes, T. (1967) *Poetry in the Making*: Faber & Faber
6 Godwin, F. J. in *Teachers World*: quoted as publisher's blurb for Clegg, A. B. (1964) *Op. Cit.*
7 Arnold, M. (1888) *Essays In Criticism*: originally in 'The Study of Poetry' (1880) published as the General Introduction to *The English Poets* ed. T. H. Ward
8 Protherough, R. (1978) 'When In Doubt Write A Poem': *English In Education* Vol. 12, No. 1
9 Treble, H. A. (1927) *The Teaching of English in Primary Schools*: Oxford
10 Froome, S. (1975) Note of Dissent appended to *A Language for Life*, the Report of the Bullock Committee: HMSO
11 Thomas, H. (1979) Unpublished interviews with teachers obtained in the course of research for an M.Litt. thesis, Oxford University Department of Educational Studies
12 Doughty, P. (1966) 'Teaching Poetry': *NATE Bulletin* 3/1
13 Britton, J. (1975) *The Development of Writing Abilities 11–18*: Macmillan

14 Ross, M. (1975) *Arts and the Adolescent*: Schools Council Working Paper 54
Witkin, R. (1974) *The Intelligence of Feeling*: Heinemann
15 Holbrook, D. (1979) *English For Meaning*: NFER, p. 62
16 DES (1975) *A Language For Life*, the Report of the Bullock Committee: HMSO, p. 135
17 Ibid. p. 137
18 Inglis, F. *The Englishness Of English Teaching*: Longman, p. 89
19 Lawrence, D. H. (1932) 'What Have They Done To You?' in *More Pansies*
20 Bourdieu, P. (1974) 'School As a Conservative Force' in Egglestone, S. J. (ed.) *Contemporary Research In the Sociology of Education*: Methuen
21 Auden, W. H. and Garrett, J. (1935) *The Poet's Tongue*: Bell
22 Thomas, H. (1979) *Op. Cit.*
23 Ibid.
24 Baldwin, M. (1959) *Poetry Without Tears*: Routledge & Kegan Paul
25 Strong, L. A. G. (1948) 'Poetry In The School' in *The Teaching of English In Schools* (ed. V. de Sola Pinto): Macmillan
26 Benton, M. (1978) 'Poetry For Children: A Neglected Art': *Children's Literature In Education* Vol. 9, No. 3, p. 113
27 Yarlott, G. and Harpin, W. S. (1972/3) '1000 Responses to English Literature': *Educational Research* 13.1 and 13.2
28 Abbs, P. (1976) *Root And Blossom*: Heinemann
29 Yarlott, G. and Harpin, W. S. (1972/3) *Op. Cit.*
30 Doughty, P. (1966) *Op. Cit.*
31 Oakley, A. J. (1981) 'A Survey of the Teaching of Poetry to Children between the Ages of 10–13 in 43 Primary, Middle and Secondary Schools in the E. Dorset Area.' Unpublished MA (Ed.) Dissertation, University of Southampton
32 DES (1982) *Language Performance in School: Secondary Survey Report No. 1*: HMSO p. 54ff.
33 Ibid p. 62

Chapter 2

1 Barnes, D. and Todd, F. (1977) *Communicating and Learning in Small Groups*: Routledge & Kegan Paul
   Barnes, D. (1976) *From Communication to Curriculum*: Penguin Books
2 Hughes, T. (1967) *Poetry in the Making*: Faber & Faber
   Holbrook, D. (1961) *English for Maturity*: Cambridge University Press
   Brownjohn, S. (1980) *Does It Have To Rhyme?*: Hodder & Stoughton
   Clegg, A. B. (1964) *The Excitement of Writing*: Chatto & Windus
   Holbrook, D. (1964) *The Secret Places*: Cambridge University Press
   Langdon, M. (1961) *Let The Children Write*: Longman
3 Brownjohn, S. (1982) *What Rhymes with Secret?*: Hodder & Stoughton
4 Doughty, P. (1966) 'Teaching Poetry': *NATE Bulletin* 3/1
5 Thomas, H. (1979) Unpublished interviews with teachers obtained in the course of research for an M.Litt thesis, Oxford University Department of Educational Studies
6 McGough, R. (1976) *In the Glassroom*: Jonathan Cape
7 Eliot, T. S. (1940) *Old Possum's Book of Practical Cats*: Faber & Faber
8 Hughes, T. (1967) *Meet My Folks!* Faber & Faber
9 Haigh, G. (1984) 'Resources for Poetry Teaching': *Times Educational Supplement* 9/3/84

Chapter 3

1 For example Britton, J. (1969) 'Talking to Learn' in *Language, The Learner and The School*, Barnes, Britton and Rosen: Penguin Books
   NATE/Schools Council (1971) *Children As Readers*, Bulletin 7
   Barnes, D. Churley, P. and Thompson, C. (1971) '*Group Talk and Literary Response: English In Education*' Vol. 5, No. 3
   Barnes, D. (1976) *From Communication to Curriculum*: Penguin Books
   Barnes, D. and Todd, F. (1977) *Communication and Learning in Small Groups*: Routledge & Kegan Paul
   Rosen, C. and Rosen H. (1973) *The Language of Primary School Children*: Penguin Books
   DES (1975) *A Language for Life*, the Report of the Bullock Committee: HMSO
   Wade, B. (1981) 'Assessing Pupils' Contributions In Appreciating A Poem': *Journal Of Education For Teaching* Vol. 7, No. 1
2 Yarlott, G. and Harpin, W. S. (1972/73) '1000

Responses to English Literature': *Educational Research* 13.1 and 13.2.
3 DES (1975) *Op. Cit.*, 9. 24
4 DES (1975) *Op. Cit.*, 9.24
5 DES (1975) *Op. Cit.*, 9.21
6 Hughes, T. (1976) In *Season Song*: Faber & Faber
7 Schools Council (1979) *Learning through Talking*, 11–16 Working Paper 64: Evans/Methuen
8 Seamus Heaney in a letter quoted by Bernard Harrison in Harrison, B. 'Poetry and the Language of Feeling': *Tract* No. 27
9 Britton, J. (1969) 'Talking to Learn' in *Language, The Learner and The School*, Barnes, Britton and Rosen: Penguin Books
10 Strong, L. A. G. (1946) 'Poetry In The School' in *The Teaching of English in Schools* (ed. V. de Sola Pinto): Macmillan
11 DES (1975) *Op. Cit.*, 4.7
12 Bruner, J. (1966) *Towards a Theory of Instruction*: Harvard University Press
13 Lawrence, D. H. 'Preface' to *Chariot of the Sun*, Harry Crosby: In E. D. Macdonald (ed.) *Phoenix*, Heinemann, p. 255
14 Fuller, R. (1976) 'The Influence of Children on Books': The Sidney Robbins Memorial Fund Lecture: *Children's Literature in Education* No. 20
15 Dewey, J. (1958) *Art As Experience*: Putnam
16 Muir, E. quoted by Mathieson, M. in 'The Problem of Poetry' (1980): *Use of English* 31/2
17 Rosen, C. and Rosen, H. (1973) *The Language of Primary School Children*: Penguin Books
18 DES/APU (1982) *Language Performance in Schools*: Secondary Survey Report No. 1: HMSO
19 Bruner, J. (1972) 'Towards A Disciplined Intuition' in *The Relevance of Education*: Allen & Unwin
20 Fox, G. and Merrick, B. (1981) 'Thirty-Six Things To Do With A Poem': *Children's Literature in Education* Vol. 12, No. 1
21 Hughes, T. (1967) 'Capturing Animals' in *Poetry in the Making*: Faber & Faber
22 Iser, W. (1978) *The Act of Reading*: Routledge & Kegan Paul
23 Murray, G. (1975) 'Poetry In The Classroom': *English In Education* Vol. 9, No. 3
24 Holland, N. (1968 and 1975) *The Dynamics of Literary Response*: W. W. Norton

Chapter 4

1 Tarleton, R. (1983) 'Children's Thinking About Poetry': *NATE News*, Summer
2 Calouste Gulbenkian Foundation (1982) *The Arts In Schools*: Gulbenkian Foundation, p. 11
3 Coleridge, S. T. (1817) *Biographia Literaria*, p. 150

4 Abbs, P. (1982) *English Within the Arts*: Hodder & Stoughton, p. 61

5 Rosenblatt, L. (1978) *The Reader, the Text, the Poem*: Southern Illinois University Press, Carbondale and Edwardsville, Feffer and Sons p. 142

6 Leavis, F. R. (1947) *Scrutiny* XV, 1

7 Witkin, R. (1974) *The Intelligence of Feeling*: Heinemann

8 Rosenblatt, L. (1978) *Op. Cit.*, p. 146

9 Barnes, D. (1976) *From Communication to Curriculum*: Penguin Books

10 Whitehead, F. (1966) *The Disappearing Dais*: Chatto & Windus, p. 93

11 Rosenblatt, L. (1978) *Op. Cit.*, pp. 104−105

12 Munro, H. 'Milk For The Cat': Duckworth

13 Heaney, S. (1966) 'Death of A Naturalist' from *Death of A Naturalist*: Faber & Faber

14 Burgess, A. (1982) *This Man and his Music*: Hutchinson, p. 25

15 Skelton, R. (1978) *Poetic Truth*: Heinemann, p. 76

16 Wade, B. (1981) 'Assessing Pupils' Contributions In Appreciating A Poem': *The Journal Of Education For Teaching* Vol. 7, No. 1

17 Squire, J. R. (1964) *Responses Of Adolescents To Four Short Stories*: Urbana, Illinois; NCTE

18 Barnes, D. and Todd, F. (1977) *Communicating and Learning in Small Groups*: Routledge & Kegan Paul

19 Harding, D. W. (1937) 'The Role of the Onlooker': *Scrutiny* VI, 3

20 Rosenblatt, L. (1978) *Op. Cit.*

21 Holland, N. (1975) *Five Readers Reading*: Yale University Press, p. 131

22 O'Malley, R. (1969) 'Poetry' in Thompson, D. (ed.) *Directions In The Teaching Of English*, Cambridge University Press

Chapter 5

1 Richards, I. A. (1943) *How to Read a Page*: Routledge & Kegan Paul

2 Brooks, C. and Penn Warren, R. (1976) *Understanding Poetry*: Holt, Rinehart, Winston, 4th edn, p. 11

3 Holbrook, D. (1962) *Thieves and Angels*: Cambridge University Press

4 May, B. (1984) *Developing Tray*: MEP for BBC B or RML380Z distributed to all LEAs (freely copiable)

5 Govier, H. (1983) 'Primary Language Development' in *Acorn User*

6 Benton, M. G. and Benton, P. (1971) *Touchstones 4*: Hodder & Stoughton, pp. 28−29

7 Phythian, B. (ed.) (1970) *Considering Poetry*: Hodder & Stoughton

8 Brooks, C. and Penn Warren, R. (1976) *Op. Cit.*

9 Benton, M. G. and Benton, P. (1967−71) *Touchstones 1−5*; (1979−82) *Watchwords 1−3*; (1975) *Poetry Workshop*; all published by Hodder & Stoughton

10 Hughes, T. (1967) *Poetry in the Making*: Faber & Faber

11 Brownjohn, S. (1980) *Does It Have To Rhyme?*: Hodder & Stoughton
Brownjohn, S. (1982) *What Rhymes with Secret?*: Hodder & Stoughton

12 Witkin, R. (1974) *The Intelligence of Feeling*: Heinemann

APPENDIX

Questions for English Departments to ask Themselves

It is usual at this point to include a full copy of any questionnaire used in research. Bearing in mind the likely general readership of this book, it is probably more helpful to present it in a form that can be of some practical use to teachers in schools.

Some of the questions from the survey described in Chapter 2 have been found by a number of English departments to be a useful starting point for a departmental meeting to discuss their own practice in teaching poetry. Therefore, instead of printing a full blown version of the whole questionnaire, I have chosen a selection of questions designed to highlight certain attitudes and approaches. Poetry teaching is a notoriously difficult subject on which to focus and the framework offered here seems to help teachers surface their own feelings and clarify their thinking.

Answers to Sections A and D should be based on the individual teacher's general experience of teaching poetry. For the remainder, Sections B, C, E and F, it is suggested that teachers should select *one* class from each year group they teach in the current school year and complete those questions with that specific class in mind.

Each teacher should complete the questionnaire independently and, where appropriate, jot down any reasons for their views or their practice.

Discussing the results (in small groups, naturally!) can be most illuminating: it can also be for some a threatening experience. It is important that people should feel secure enough to be honest in their replies which will, of course, be theirs to offer in general discussion *or not* as they wish. Nobody should be put in the position of *having* to reveal their answers to colleagues.

Section A

Basing your responses on your general experience of poetry teaching, please complete the following statements. (Delete as appropriate):

1 I think it is (1) very important (2) important (3) not particularly important to read and discuss poetry in class with my pupils because . . .

2 I think it is (1) very important (2) important (3) not particularly important for my pupils to write poetry in class or at home because . . .

3 The main problems/worries I have about teaching poetry are . . .

Section B

Choose *one* class from each year group you
teach in the current school year and complete the following questions with that
particular class in mind.

4 How often, on average, do you teach poetry?*

	1	2	3	4	5	6
Age group	More than once/week	About once/week	Once a fortnight	Once a month	Once in 4–8 weeks	Less frequently
11–12						
12–13						
13–14						
14–15						
15–16						

5 How long, on average, do you spend teaching poetry on each occasion?

	1	2	3	4	5	6
Age group	Less than 10 minutes	10–20 minutes	20–30 minutes	30–40 minutes	40–50 minutes	More than 50 minutes
11–12						
12–13						
13–14						
14–15						
15–16						

* The expression 'teach poetry' is used here and
throughout as a convenient shorthand and should be
taken to mean any activity, of whatever duration, involving reading poetry, discussing poetry, writing
poetry or writing *about* poetry.

Section C

Please refer only to the classes already selected by you and to the current school year. Please use the blank space beneath each question to comment on or give reasons for your answers if possible.

	Age group	1 Always/almost always	2 Often	3 Sometimes	4 Rarely	5 Never
6 Do you arrange poetry as a separate lesson with your classes?	11–12					
	12–13					
	13–14					
	14–15					
	15–16					
7 Do you ask pupils to discuss a poem in small groups after reading?	11–12					
	12–13					
	13–14					
	14–15					
	15–16					
8 Do you ask for related written work when teaching poetry?	11–12					
	12–13					
	13–14					
	14–15					
	15–16					
9 Does this take the form of asking pupils to write a poem?	11–12					
	12–13					
	13–14					
	14–15					
	15–16					

	Age group	1 Always/almost always	2 Often	3 Sometimes	4 Rarely	5 Never
10 Do you ask pupils to write some kind of critical analysis or response to the poem?	11–12					
	12–13					
	13–14					
	14–15					
	15–16					
11 Do you ask pupils to copy out poems by published writers?	11–12					
	12–13					
	13–14					
	14–15					
	15–16					
12 Do you write your own poems alongside your pupils in class?	11–12					
	12–13					
	13–14					
	14–15					
	15–16					
13 Do you show any of your own poems to your classes?	11–12					
	12–13					
	13–14					
	14–15					
	15–16					

	Age group	1 Always/almost always	2 Often	3 Sometimes	4 Rarely	5 Never

14 Do you correct spelling and punctuation errors in poems written by pupils?

Age group	Always/almost always	Often	Sometimes	Rarely	Never
11–12					
12–13					
13–14					
14–15					
15–16					

15 Do you suggest alterations in vocabulary or technical handling of verse in poems written by pupils

Age group	Always/almost always	Often	Sometimes	Rarely	Never
11–12					
12–13					
13–14					
14–15					
15–16					

16 Do you ask pupils to produce second or third drafts of their poems?

Age group	Always/almost always	Often	Sometimes	Rarely	Never
11–12					
12–13					
13–14					
14–15					
15–16					

17 Do you, after reading and discussion of a poem, re-read it with the class?

Age group	Always/almost always	Often	Sometimes	Rarely	Never
11–12					
12–13					
13–14					
14–15					
15–16					

	Age group	Always/almost always 1	Often 2	Sometimes 3	Rarely 4	Never 5
18 Do you ask pupils to learn any poetry by heart?	11–12					
	12–13					
	13–14					
	14–15					
	15–16					
19 Do you use poetry for the purpose of choral speaking?	11–12					
	12–13					
	13–14					
	14–15					
	15–16					
20 Do you 'publish' examples of pupils' own poetry either by wall display or by duplicating collections of their own work etc.?	11–12					
	12–13					
	13–14					
	14–15					
	15–16					
21 Do you give a mark or grade on poems written by pupils?	11–12					
	12–13					
	13–14					
	14–15					
	15–16					

Age group	1 Always/almost always	2 Often	3 Sometimes	4 Rarely	5 Never
11–12					
12–13					
13–14					
14–15					
15–16					

22 Do pupils show you their own poems written voluntarily in their own leisure time?

Section D

Basing your responses on your general experience of poetry teaching, for each of the statements below circle one of the numbers to show how strongly you disagree or agree with the statement.

	Disagree				*Agree*
23 Teaching poetry is one of the aspects of English I enjoy most.	1	2	3	4	5
24 I find it difficult to know when and how to introduce technical terms.	1	2	3	4	5
25 The teaching of poetry is at the heart of English teaching.	1	2	3	4	5
26 I don't know enough about poetry myself to feel confident when teaching it.	1	2	3	4	5
27 Teachers should write poetry themselves from time to time if they ask pupils to do so.	1	2	3	4	5
28 I find it difficult to read poetry aloud well.	1	2	3	4	5
29 Poetry does not really interest me very much.	1	2	3	4	5
30 The teaching of poetry is less important than most other activities in English.	1	2	3	4	5
31 Writing poetry is only for the more able pupil.	1	2	3	4	5

Section E

32 Please give details of any single volumes of verse by particular poets that have proved notably successful either in whole or in part with your pupils. As before, tick the appropriate age groups.

33 Please recommend up to *four* poems that you have found particularly suitable for and successful with classes you have taught this year

Section F

In the questions that follow please tick *one* box for each age group that you teach this year to show how strongly you disagree or agree with each statement. *Continue to refer only to the classes selected by you previously and to the current school year. Please use the blank space to comment further if you wish.*

Age group	1 Disagree	2	3	4	5 Agree
11–12					
12–13					
13–14					
14–15					
15–16					

34 I should prefer to teach poetry more often than I do with this age group

Age group	1	2	3	4	5
11–12					
12–13					
13–14					
14–15					
15–16					

35 Most pupils of this age group dislike poetry

Age group	1	2	3	4	5
11–12					
12–13					
13–14					
14–15					
15–16					

36 I do not feel as confident about teaching poetry to this age group as I do about teaching other aspects of English.

Age group	1	2	3	4	5
11–12					
12–13					
13–14					
14–15					
15–16					

37 Poetry is of greater interest to the girls than to the boys in this age group

Age group	1	2	3	4	5
11–12					
12–13					
13–14					
14–15					
15–16					

	Age group	1 *Disagree*	2	3	4	5 *Agree*
38 I usually enjoy poetry lessons with this group	11–12					
	12–13					
	13–14					
	14–15					
	15–16					

	Age group	1	2	3	4	5
39 I find it difficult to interest pupils of this age in writing poetry	11–12					
	12–13					
	13–14					
	14–15					
	15–16					

	Age group	1	2	3	4	5
40 It is difficult to find poems suitable for my class at this age.	11–12					
	12–13					
	13–14					
	14–15					
	15–16					

	Age group	1	2	3	4	5
41 Pupils of this age group often seem willing to express feelings in poetry that they do not readily express in other forms of writing.	11–12					
	12–13					
	13–14					
	14–15					
	15–16					

	1	2	3	4	5
Age group	Disagree				Agree

42 Teaching poetry to this age group puts them off it rather than increases their enjoyment

Age group	Disagree				Agree
11—12					
12—13					
13—14					
14—15					
15—16					

43 My pupils in this age group are generally unwilling to discuss their personal response to a poem

Age group					
11—12					
12—13					
13—14					
14—15					
15—16					

44 My pupils in this age group generally tend to regard poetry as 'cissy'

Age group					
11—12					
12—13					
13—14					
14—15					
15—16					